# DAVID
# SILVA

## EL MAGO

# DAVID SILVA EL MAGO

## A DECADE OF MAGIC

**Reach** Sport

# #21

Written and edited by: David Clayton
Head Photographer: Victoria Haydn
Assistant Club Photographers: Tom Flathers & Matt McNulty
Additional imagery with thanks to Getty Images, PA Images.

Special thanks to: Javier Brusés Manresa, Anna Gil, Francesc Guimera, John De Caux, Chris Bailey and CityTV, Gavin Johnson, Will Beedles, Daniel Fresco.

And gracias to David Silva for supporting this project, his family and friends and, of course, Sergio Aguero for the foreword.

*Watch 'Made in Gran Canaria' on City+ if you haven't already.*

First published in Great Britain and Ireland in 2020 by Reach Sport,
part of Reach PLC Ltd, 5 St Paul's Square, Liverpool, L3 9SJ
One Canada Square, Canary Wharf, London, E15 5AP.

Executive Editor: Paul Dove. Executive Art Editor: Rick Cooke
Production Editor: Adam Oldfield. Design: Mark Frances, Colin Harrison.
Translation: Thanks to Philip Dickinson.

ISBN: 9781911613534

Printed and bound by Bell & Bain Ltd

"David Silva would walk into any City team of any era. He is in my personal greatest all-time XI and is just fantastic to watch"

— Colin Bell

# CONTENTS

# SERGIO AGUERO

# David Silva

## is the beacon of
## Manchester City

**T**o 'assist' means to give, to deliver, to tag along.

All of that becomes more valuable if you can do it in a natural, genuine way. When you factor in the competitiveness of the modern football scene, a whole new dimension is added – it illustrates the generosity of those who assist. That's who you are, David.

What really enhances your accomplishments is that what you do on the playing field is a truthful reflection of your personality outside of it.

That's the real magic, the kind of magic those who are close to you have witnessed throughout the years. The kind of magic that football fans enjoy when they watch you play.

When someone can break past the Club lines and achieve recognition from the supporters of other teams at a global level, that's when a legend is born. That's what you are, David – a legend.

And while you receive much praise, it's never gone to your head – you are still an ordinary, down-to-earth person who keeps an open heart for his country and his family.

You have made assisting your biggest virtue – your drive to share, and to bringing the best out of others.

There has been a before and an after for Manchester City since you were here. For that, and in the name of all of those who are part of this Club, you have my endless gratitude – you've made us all bigger with your talent and your humility.

I learned a lot from you, we all do, every single day.

You're going to be missed, but you'll always be with us.

For each picture-perfect assist, for each subtle pass, for each cunning play, in each goal, that's where you'll be.

When anyone wants to learn what it really means to put the team over the self, that's where you'll be too. That's your true magic. You've empowered the team with it, and it will be the beacon that will light us all forever.

# Gracias, Mago

'**E**l *Mago – a Decade of Magic*' is not an autobiography. It isn't an in-depth analytical study of a very gifted footballer, either. What this book is, is a celebration of one of the Club's greatest footballers and most loyal servants.

In it, we track David's footballing life from the small fishing village he grew up in to the present day, plus everything that happened in-between in words and pictures. It's been an incredible journey and one that has seen David become that most rare of things in the football world – universally loved and respected, by not only his adoring legion of Manchester City fans, but by supporters of other teams, opposing players and managers and just about anyone who has ever seen him play.

He is a superstar, but a reluctant one. It's never been about him and what he's done, just what he can do with a football and how he can help those around him.

Humble, gifted and the one constant behind a revolution that made Manchester City a domestic tour de force; he has won just about everything there is to win in the game at Club and international level.

City fans across the world will agree that to have had David Silva working his magic in sky blue for a decade is worth any trophy on the planet.

From every City fan, gracias mago.

And don't be a stranger…

# The boy from Arguineguín

*(El niño de Arguineguín)*

Arguineguin, temporada '97-'98

# "WHEN YOU'RE GOOD, EVERYONE PICKS YOU..."

**F**ew City fans paid much notice to the scorer of the Valencia goal in the Thomas Cook Trophy season opener in August 2007. The game, no more than a glorified friendly against invited opposition, was a chance for the fans to see any new signings that had been made during the summer, and on this occasion, there were several arrivals making their first appearance as recently appointed manager Sven-Goran Eriksson attempted to assemble a squad that was capable of challenging for silverware.

In total, there were seven new signings for the crowd to run their eye over, but in a generally underwhelming match, it would be the slightly framed Valencia No.21 who would score the only goal of the game after 10 minutes to give the La Liga side a 1-0 victory. As the scorer's name – David Silva – was announced to the half-full City of Manchester Stadium, nobody could have realised what the future held and just how influential the 21-year-old attacking midfielder would become to Manchester City.

Within three years, Silva would swap the Valencia orange for the

City fans' first sight of Silva came in the orange of Valencia as the then 21-year-old settled a 2007 August friendly at the City of Manchester Stadium

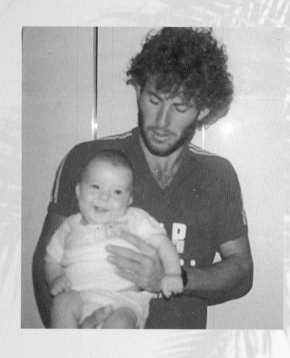

# David Josué Jiménez Silva

Manchester sky blue and begin to rewrite the history books during an incredible decade of success at Club, international and personal level. For many, he would become the greatest player City ever signed. Quite a statement, given the competition, but one with plenty of gravitas.

But the start of that era was still some time ahead, and plenty would happen for both the player and Manchester City in the intervening period, and there is quite a back story to fill in, first.

David Josue Jimenez Silva was born on 8 January 1986 in the Gran Canarian fishing village of Arguineguín, which lies on the southern tip of the island and has both a beach and a harbour. An ideal place for any child to grow up. Year-round tourists are abundant in the picturesque port with Norwegians in particular attracted to the peace and tranquil atmosphere.

His parents, Fernando and Eva were respected local citizens and his father was a municipal police officer. Slightly built – small even, for his age – David grew up in the idyllic surrounds of a loving family, warm sunshine and the glorious Atlantic Ocean as his playground.

"The weather is nice and warm virtually all-year round and I'm very lucky to have been brought up in such a beautiful place," said David. "I am very proud to be from Gran Canaria. I like to go home

**Growing up in the fishing village of Arguineguín, on the Spanish isle of Gran Canaria, Silva was surrounded by a sea of blue, a precursor to life at the City of Manchester Stadium**

whenever I have the time. It is a very multi-cultural place and great for tourists from all over the world. Plenty of English people go there and seem to enjoy it. As a kid, Las Palmas, who were based on the opposite side of the island, were my team and I would go to watch them whenever I could."

Like many Arguineguín kids, he loved to play football, fish, barbecue, swim and spend time at the beach, but if he had to choose one hobby over all the others, it was football.

"You don't learn to play football. It's not like school, where someone can sit you down and teach you how to do this or do that," said David. "You have to know how to play and love playing, then you learn new things. I suppose I just picked it up like all other children do, playing with my friends. We played wherever we could."

He was obsessed with the game from the moment he could walk and he was never without a ball at his feet or under his arm.

Proud parents: Father Fernando Jiménez and mother Eva Silva with a very young David (who already has his hands on a trophy!)

"I bought him a toy truck and he never looked at it," recalled David's mother. "It was just footballs, boots, shirts, all those things."

His teacher at the local junior school, Inmaculada Garcia, added: "They'd play tournaments at break time. Football, of course. He was always one of the kids everyone would pick. When you're good, everyone picks you. And David was very good."

Union Deportiva Las Palmas, the major Club of Gran Canaria, were David's team and whenever possible, he would make the near-30-mile trip with his father to the 21,000-capacity Estadio Insular ('Island Stage') to watch his heroes play. During David's

Making his way: David
at the Uli Stielike training
camp in Maspalomas

At the Estadio Heliodoro Rodriguez Lopez in Tenerife ahead of a Gran Canaria v Tenerife regional match

Already making a name for himself – picking up an award

"From the very beginning you could see he did things differently from other kids; on the pitch, he'd see things other kids didn't see"

formative years, Las Palmas would drift between the Segunda Division and Segunda Division B (the Spanish third tier) during a troubled period in their relatively short history. Las Palmas were formed after the merger of five Gran Canaria clubs in 1949 in a bid to stop the exodus of talented islanders over to mainland Spain to pursue their career.

The fledgling Club's golden era had been the team that played between 1967 and 1969 and had managed third and second place finishes consecutively in La Liga. Nonetheless, the team proved a great success and united the island as never before, with the Gran Canarian people finally united behind one cause. For the young David Silva, like his father, they were his team and he dreamed of one day representing them.

"The first memory we have – just like we see now with his son, Mateo – is with a football by his side," said David's uncle, Jose Manuel Jimenez. "Wherever he went, he'd always have a ball under his arm. He was always breaking things left, right and centre, with his grandma always angry with David and friends. Something his father would always say was that he would retire on this kid's talent. And look what happened..."

But like any loving grandparent, his grandmother would put up with it. She'd feed him and his friends no matter what time of the day he'd turn up, and if he drove her mad in the house, she'd roll up an old newspaper and let them play in the yard for hours on end with it.

His father, a skilful amateur player himself, would take David to watch him play and most of his younger years were spent either playing or watching football. As soon as his young son could walk, Fernando Jimenez took him along to watch training.

"From the very beginning you could see he did things differently from other kids," said Fernando.

"As he got a little bigger, he was on the pitch, he'd see things other kids didn't see and it would be a case of him and another ten kids whenever he played. The opposition coach would always come over after the game and say: 'that boy has ability – he will go far.'"

Aythami Artiles, one of David's closest childhood friends and a future Las Palmas player, remembers his talented buddy wasn't always flavour of the month in the neighbourhood due to his football obsession, which often drove those living close by to distraction.

"To be honest, we had a lot of problems with the neighbours," he smiled. "We'd always be smacking the ball against doors, windows, cars or whatever and it didn't go down too well! We lived right next to each other. Nothing out of the ordinary, but to us it was very special. We'd have dinner together, we'd play, have sleepovers, get up at the same time and we played in the same junior team.

"When we were on the same junior side, I knew what my role was in the team. I was the ball-winner and he'd be the match-winner. Because of his ability, he always played in higher age groups. That obviously helped him because he was a boy

Childhood friend Aythami Artiles remembers days he and David spent infuriating locals when playing football

playing against men. Eventually, he couldn't play for us because he was underage.

"He was in the group below, the U11/12s. So thanks to a friend of his, he played with someone else's registration form. He had the same haircut and they looked similar. On the day David played we were 4-0 up and the goalkeeper's mother, who knew him, complained. She was saying, 'David can't play! It's not fair!' But we said: 'Wait a minute, he's a year younger, so what difference does it

Pictured with team-mates, David *(centre)* celebrates a trophy won with San Fernando at Maspalomas. David and his team-mates won all the regional trophies with San Fernando, including this one after beating Tenerife 4-0 in the final – David scored twice

David is pictured (bottom right) at the Arguineguín Football Ground. His ambitions of being a goalkeeper soon changed after being influenced by the talents of Norwegian attacking midfielder Michael Laudrup *(above)*. Pictured right: David with hero Juan Carlos Valerón and his brother Miguel Angel Valerón

make?' But we swapped his shirt and put on another boy who was allowed to play."

A very young David Silva had first wanted to be a goalkeeper and was happy to take the gloves in the knockabouts with his friends and school matches when he first started playing. But even as young as he was, the fact was that he physically wasn't built to be a keeper. He would need to have had a tremendous growth spurt to achieve his early aspirations. But things were about to change and targets reset.

"Juan Carlos Valeron quickly became my idol," said David. "He'd played with my dad and his brother Miguel-Angel. He was from Arguineguín and played for my team, Las Palmas, for a while. Valeron was my inspiration and, later, when I got to know him, he was a fantastic person, too."

La Liga matches were often on TV in the Silva household and that meant regular matches involving Spanish giants Real Madrid or Catalan aristocrats Barcelona – and while Valeron was his idol at the time, another player had caught David's eye – that of brilliant Barcelona playmaker Michael Laudrup. The supremely talented Dane was one of the world's most skilful footballers and one of La Liga's biggest stars. He had joined Barça from Juventus in 1989 and would spend five years at the Camp Nou and, controversially, another two years with Madrid after a falling out with coach Johan Cruyff.

For seven years, Laudrup made headlines in Spanish football and watching him whenever he could, was an awestruck David Silva who had by then long since metaphorically tossed his goalkeeper gloves to one side in a bid to remodel himself on aspects of Valeron's game and elements of Laudrup's.

"Laudrup was my hero," said David. "He was a brilliant, skilful player and I suppose, apart from Valeron, if I studied anyone closely, it would have to have been him."

David with
Club Deportivo
Arguineguín, aged
around 10

He couldn't have chosen two better role models and as David studied the elegant, skilful and strong Dane, and along with the strengths and abilities of local legend Valeron, his own unique style began to emerge…

In 1992, Union Deportiva San Fernando were formed as a football club in the nearby resort of Maspalomas and just a 10-minute drive from Arguineguín. David joined the newly-created Gran Canarian side at youth team level. It was at San Fernando that he started to blossom, regularly playing with different age groups and more than holding his own. For his size, he was strong as an ox and he soon discovered a love of dribbling past bigger players and using his vision and skill to create chances for others. His trademark spin away from trouble was straight from the handbook of Valeron, who developed a method that kept him away from defenders snapping at his heels.

David's trademark turn is something he shares with Valerón, who used it to great effect during his playing days

Valeron can see the similarities in David's game to the ones he had during his playing days, saying: "People have spoken about that 'classic turn' he does – that is something I also liked to do. I think it was a defensive mechanism I used to protect myself from players that were more physical than me."

That David loved his home and that he dreamed of playing for Las Palmas one day was without question, but the fact was he was outgrowing local football and his ability demanded a grander stage. His father also believed his son should have the opportunity of a bigger and better stage to perform on and agreed to take him for a trial at Real Madrid.

"We had good players in the team I played in and we were winning everything," recalled David. "We'd go to Tenerife to play against the champions there. Then, with the Canary Islands team, we'd go over to the mainland where more people would see you.

When more people see you, you have more options and when I was 12, I was invited to spend a week in Madrid."

He travelled to mainland Spain with his father for a trial with *Los Blancos*, then under the tutelage of Vicente del Bosque. The trial went well and David showed flashes of the talent that had beguiled so many, but the timing wasn't right. His father Fernando accepted Real Madrid's decision not to take him on straight away, but rather keep a close eye on David's progress. Fernando recalled: "Del Bosque looked at him. He said, 'the kid has ability, potential. He has vision', but added he was still very young. It was true he was only 12. So, I said, 'I've not brought him here to stay. If you think he's a player you might be interested in, he can go back to his town and you can monitor him.' So the agreement with Del Bosque was that David would return the following year to Madrid."

Real Madrid had missed their opportunity, and it's fair to say it is one they came to regret in the years that followed.

Family were always extremely supportive and very proud of David as he started to make a name for himself

David said: "After that, I didn't go again to Madrid. They'd call me year after year, but I didn't go. I went back to my town where I played until I was 14. That's when Valencia contacted me…"

Valencia scout Jose Jiménez had been alerted that there were a number of promising Gran Canarians who might be worth taking a look at. Jiménez trusted his judgement and took the opportunity to take a closer look at the four youngsters who had been recommended to him. He recalled: "There was an agent who worked with us on the island. He'd keep us informed about which players were standing out over there. He asked if we'd like to take four players for a trial. All of them were fantastic. Silva was a cut above."

After that, things moved quickly…

David stood out when four young hopefuls from Gran Canaria went to Valencia for a trial

# I get knocked down, but I get up again...

*(Me derriban, pero me levanto de nuevo ...)*

# "WE'VE GOT A SPECIAL PLAYER ON OUR HANDS, HERE..."

t was a daunting prospect to live away from his family, friends and everything he knew to pursue his dream, but the 14-year-old David Silva knew that if he wanted to make it, he would have to accept Valencia's offer.

*Los Che* were one of European football's best teams when he arrived in 2000, having finished third in La Liga while also reaching their first Champions League final (which they lost to Real Madrid). They were a club on the rise, attempting to disrupt the Barça/Real domination. It was a golden era for Valencia, the best in the club's history. Like David, head coach Rafael Benitez had just joined and also left the Canary Islands where he had taken Tenerife into La Liga after one season in charge. Whether that resonated with the 40-year-old or not is unclear, but he would keep a close eye on the teenager's progress.

But first, David had to fight the loneliness and homesickness that, at times, overwhelmed the youngster. He recalled: "Because I was very young at the time, it was difficult for me.

David knew that he had to leave home to follow his dream but it wasn't easy adapting to a new life. He is pictured here in 2000 – his first year with Valencia

David during trials with
Spain Under-15s

# "He was only 14 and was on his own there. You could see he was down and he'd be crying"

"It's a big move to go to a big city, and the Canary Islands are away from the mainland. It was a tough decision to move, but it was too good an opportunity to turn down. Now they've got mobile phones with FaceTime where you can see your family every day, but those first few months, that first year was tough. I suffered a great deal."

His father made the exciting yet painful journey with his son to Valencia, knowing full well he would be returning home without David.

"I went with him to Valencia on that day," said Fernando. "When I left him at the training ground, I started crying because he was looking at me as if to say, 'You're leaving me here, right?' I felt so sorry for him, but in the end I carried on walking and didn't look back."

Though David was determined to succeed, there was a point, a few weeks into his time with Valencia, where something needed to change. He was too close to his family to be without them and something had to give.

Eva Silva, his mother, was heartbroken every time she spoke to her son on the phone. "Each time I spoke to him I'd be in tears. It broke my heart," she said. "Because he was only 14, and he was on his own there. You could see he was down and he'd be crying."

David with a trophy awarded for being the best player of the Spanish National Championship, first round

His family tried to encourage him to tough it out, but his grandmother felt he needed more than supportive words.

"I'd say, 'my boy's not right, he's in a bad way. Either his mother or his father needs to go there and be with him," she said. Eva Silva had seen enough.

After discussions with David's father, she said: 'Right, I'll go.' "I left my job, everything, and I went."

Apart from his family, David missed Arguineguin. It was his world and everything he knew and loved was there. He wasn't the first ambitious youngster to find it hard to leave behind, but his mother's arrival would make things easier. His parents were investing everything in helping David achieve his dream and, in time, his father would take on a security position at Valencia's Mestalla Stadium.

David may have been sad and lonely initially at Valencia, but for all his shyness and natural modesty, when it came to playing football, he was a completely different animal and had soon caught the attention of an agent, Amadeo Rengel, who quickly added the teenage protégé to his books.

Champions! David celebrates winning the Spanish National Football Championship – the final round was played at Maspalomas in Gran Canaria

"At that young age when we started to represent him, you could already see his technical and tactical ability," said Rengel. "You can get a feeling about how he will develop physically. But the mental attributes are the last ones to develop. These are the most difficult ones to spot in young players."

Valencia played the 14-year-old Silva in their Under-17s and Under-18s teams, and he more than held his own.

When he scored a hat-trick in the final of the Spanish equivalent of the FA Youth Cup, the media really sat up and noticed the talented 16-year-old. He was soon representing his country at Under-16, 17 and 19 youth levels, culminating in an unforgettable Under-17s World Cup when an injured Silva climbed off the bench to save his country from defeat against South Korea.

"I was injured in this World Cup," he remembered. "I had a hip problem and it was really hurting me, but they selected me. I don't know how – it was a miracle."

Trailing 2-0 to South Korea at the break, his coach took a risk and brought on Silva who was clearly in discomfort, but it proved a masterstroke as he scored an 11-minute hat-trick to secure a 3-2 victory. He would help Spain reach the final where they lost 1-0 to Brazil, but nobody was in any doubt as to who had been one of the stars of the tournament.

By now settled and happy with life, he was given an opportunity with Segunda Division reserve side Valencia B, but to further his education, it was decided he would be loaned out for the 2004/05 season. The eventual destination for the silky-skilled playmaker would raise more than a few eyebrows as he headed to the Basque Country with second tier Eibar, coached by the respected Jose Luis Mendilibar. Eibar were known as a big, physical side who relied on their brawn and team spirit rather that their technical ability. It seemed the last place a slightly built, inexperienced 18-year-old should be heading to.

Mendilibar recalls: "We were having lunch with one of the directors and when we'd finished, Javi Perez said to me: 'There's a chance of getting a left-footed Valencia player here. He's played internationally at many levels.' I said, 'Right, let's get him in.'"

David's father discovered the fitness coach at Eibar, Tony Luiz, was also from Gran Canaria and thought it would be good for

David *(bottom row, second left)* with the
Spain Under-19s at the 2004 Under-19
European Championships in Switzerland

"The typical technical
footballer is one who
never defends. You go
around them easily and
they don't track back.
Not him. He liked to run,
liked to get stuck in"

his son to have an immediate connection with a member of the coaching staff. Almost immediately, the pair hit it off and made the transition easier for the teenager.

Luiz said: "I remember the manager told me, 'One of your compatriots from the Canary Islands is going to join us.' And he says, 'It's David Silva'. And I say, 'Isn't that the kid playing at international level, the Canarian?' At that time it didn't seem to match; a talented, technical player coming into Eibar, a team with a reputation of having big, strong, powerful players."

Nobody thought Eibar was right for him. His friends and team-mates at Eibar thought he was crazy, but David was determined to make the move work. He recalled: "I got there a day before the season started. I hadn't even trained with the team, so I watched the first game from the stands. And obviously, when I saw the intensity, the way the game was played, it was clear – either I got my head down and became the guy who worked hardest, or I was never going to play there."

From day one, the inner strength and steely determination that had taken David this far emerged at his first training session, where he fought and scrapped with players twice his size, earning their respect immediately. And that of head coach Mendilibar...

"Yes he was a technical player from the Canary Islands, but he also had something else about him," said the Eibar chief.

"The typical technical footballer is one who never defends. You go around them easily and they stay there and don't track back. Not him. He wasn't about that. He liked to run, liked to get stuck in. He was different.

"He learned to get stuck in during training sessions, to train in the mud, to go in hard, to be unforgiving with his team-mates in training. And I think he was one of the hardest or a bit of a bastard in a sense when he trained.

"Despite being small he wouldn't back out of tackles. I think coming to play with us at Eibar was really good for him. I started putting him out wide, both in training and in games at the beginning, and then we realised that was wrong. He had to play centrally."

David's Las Palmas hero Valeron hadn't realised he had been doing well and progressed to senior football, so when he saw him turn out for Eibar it was case of, "David Silva? From Arguineguin?" He was delighted with his progress and better still, when he saw him toughing it out at the lower end of the Segunda Division, holding his own against wily and experienced pros who had been around the block and back, he was especially impressed.

Eibar chief Jose Luis Mendilibar recognised straight away that David had special qualities on top of his technical ability

"Eibar was a club in that period that had nothing to do with the way David played," said Valeron. "Nothing at all. And he's able to do what he did there? I said, 'We've got a special player on our hands here.'"

Opposition players and coaches were equally impressed with the teenager's unusual mix of grit and technique. He had come from nowhere but made an instant impact and earned the respect of those who maybe thought they could bully him out on the pitch or at least scare him off with one or two robust challenges.

David helped change the way Eibar played football. The tough, uncompromising aspect of their style remained, but they now had a player who could make something out of nothing and knitted the play from defence into attack.

He was a revelation and he played 35 times that season and came very close to guiding Eibar into La Liga, with the Basque side finishing fourth, just three points behind champions Cadiz and Celta Vigo and Alaves who all finished on 76 points.

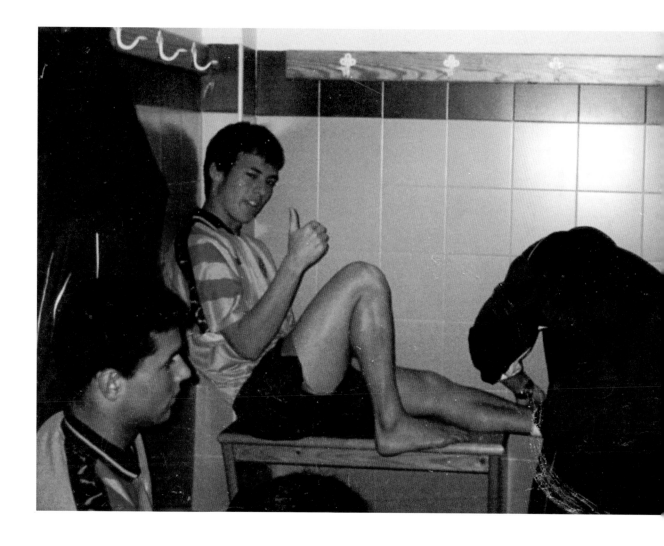

His time with the club was over and he was to return to Valencia, but *Los Che* wanted him to have another season out on loan to further expand his all-round game – but this time, with a top flight team.

David's father Fernando remembered the initial loan deal. Quique Sanchez Flores was leaving Getafe to become head coach at Valencia and David would go in the opposite direction, spending the season with Getafe. But things didn't quite go to plan…

"There's quite an interesting story here," said Fernando, "and

David enjoying life with Valencia's regional team

I'm not sure if many people are aware of it. Valencia were kind of insisting that David went to Getafe, because that year Quique Sanchez Flores had just joined Valencia, so the deal went, 'We've brought in Quique, so you can take David there.' But the doctor at Getafe said that he wasn't fit enough to play football – when he'd just played an entire season at Eibar!"

David added: "So we called Celta Vigo again to see if they were still interested. They said they were, so I joined them and it ended up being a fantastic year at Celta. I scored in one of my first few games – against Malaga – and that gave me a bit of a confidence boost and gave me that little bit extra and maybe even freed me up a bit more. From that moment on, everything was much better.

"You notice that the game is faster, almost like everyone thinks a lot more quickly. I think in the Segunda Division probably it was more about being well-organized and more physical. In Primera, everything was a lot quicker. In terms of my own game, I had learned to compete physically in my time with Eibar, which, along with the other qualities I had, was really good for me. I'd always been able to react and move the ball quickly, so it was a combination for me to go on to improve a lot as a player."

With another impressive season behind him, the now 20-year-old David Silva was recalled to Valencia where new coach Sanchez Flores was keen to give him his chance. It was one that he would grasp with both hands…

David spent the 2005/06 season out on loan at Celta Vigo, scoring four goals in 34 La Liga appearances and helping the newly promoted side to an impressive sixth-place finish

*(El mago de Mestalla)*

# Magician
## of the
# Mestalla

# "WHY ARE WE LETTING HIM GO? HE'S A WONDERFUL PLAYER!"

**D**avid travelled with the rest of the Valencia squad to their pre-season training camp in Holland. After two years out on loan, he needed to break into the Valencia squad if he was to kick on again. With almost 70 appearances under his belt during his spells with Eibar and Celta Vigo, he had served his apprenticeship and was determined to impress head coach Quique Sanchez Flores, who had guided *Los Che* to a third-place La Liga finish in his first season.

Sanchez Flores was impressed and after just a few days watching the youngster, he had made his mind up. He recalled: "Well we knew that David was out on loan, first at Eibar and then Celta. We had David working with us for a week in Holland. Each time we saw him play and get a touch on the ball, we thought, 'Why are we letting him go? He's a wonderful player!'

"When David started training with us, I realised that he was a player that made everything better. He made everything simple. Each time the ball came to him, he had this outstanding ability

David scored on his Valencia home debut, a 3-0 win over Red Bull Salzburg, helping *Los Che* qualify for the group stages of the 2006/07 Champions League

to bring clarity to a situation. That's why I had no doubts about David. He made us better in a footballing sense. He gave us greater quality and he was industrious, too. He worked hard for the team. He had all the necessary qualities.

"I think there were a lot of players who helped him. I mean many players with expertise who enabled David to establish himself in the team."

The blossoming Valencia star struck up a formidable attacking partnership with David Villa in his first season

"When they demand so much and you're prepared – particularly mentally – to be honest it was great for me, and I was ready!" added David.

And ready he was. David slipped effortlessly into the Valencia team and *Los Che* were soon once again challenging for the title with Sanchez Flores reshaping his squad in the summer, blooding youngsters and making astute signings in the transfer market. Valencia would go on to finish fourth in the table and made the quarter-finals of the Champions League, with Silva forging an almost telepathic relationship with striker David Villa.

Silva played 49 games in his first full season with Valencia, scoring eight goals and making countless others. It had been a memorable campaign for him, having also won his first senior cap for Spain against Romania. But if the first season back at the Mestalla had been a dream, the second was far more turbulent with Sanchez Flores sacked in October and eventually replaced by Ronald Koeman a few weeks later.

A second successful season at Valencia followed for Silva, and he would soon make a similar impact at international level

Koeman would last until April before former club official Voro took on the role briefly ahead of Unai Emery's appointment. In total there had been four managers during 2007/08, yet Silva was continually selected, making 50 appearances and scoring seven goals.

As the turmoil bubbled away in the background at the Mestalla, Silva's talent shone like a beacon and he would do enough to earn a place in Spain's 23-man squad for the 2008 European Championship finals, though a disappointing La Liga campaign was soon forgotten as Valenica saw off Barcelona 4-3 on aggregate in the Copa del Rey semi-final before beating Getafe 3-1 in the final to lift Spanish football's most prestigious domestic cup competition.

After finishing tenth in La Liga, it was time for Euro 2008. David Villa recalled how Silva quickly became part of a Spanish revolution that would create history over a golden four-year period during which *La Roja* would end a 44-year wait to be crowned

The 2007/08 season brought Silva's first major piece of silverware, his two assists in the Copa del Rey final helping Valencia lift the coveted trophy

Silva fires home Spain's third goal against Russia, securing *La Roja's* place in the Euro 2008 final

"Without a crop of players like the one we had; we couldn't have won everything that we did. You have to make the most of that, and that's what we did with Spain"

champions in an international tournament by first claiming Euro 2008. Silva was integral during the tournament and when Spain made it to the semi-final, the world took notice as Luis Aragones' team systematically took apart Russia to win 3-0, with Silva bagging the decisive third on 82 minutes to book a place in the final against serial tournament winners Germany.

"We went through a generational change with Spain," said Villa. "We had the 'little guys' as we called them playing in the middle. We showed the world that you can win with technique in midfield, you don't need physical players. With Xavi, Iniesta and Silva we went through that generational change."

Silva added: "Without a crop of players like the one we had; we couldn't have won everything that we did. You have to make the most of that, and that's what we did with Spain. I think everything coincided in the sense that we had quite a gifted and grounded group of players who took everything and everyone on board, so they all quickly felt at ease with each other. I reckon that in any major tournament, you always need to have things going your way and have to have that bit of luck – and then really believe."

Silva was swept away with the excitement of the tournament, feeling relaxed and ready to take on the world.

He said: "I genuinely think that there was a feeling of hope and expectation. In my own case, as a lad of 20 years-old, I didn't feel any pressure at all. So all I wanted to do was to enjoy myself. I think the final against Germany was a turning point for the rest of Europe. They went, 'Look at Spain, they're playing so well and what's more they are winning too.'

"It was a historic moment just to be in the final. And it left us a step away from achieving something really special for an entire country and generation. We were totally convinced that we could win that final against Germany. And we did."

An altercation with Germany's Lukas Podolski led to David being withdrawn on 66 minutes, but by then, Fernando Torres had already scored what would prove to be the only goal of the game and win Spain their first major championship since 1964.

"The celebrations were fantastic because it was the first victory and everyone was really happy," said Silva. "When we got back to Spain, you can imagine what the fans were like. We really went for it in the celebrations – so much so that I didn't make the reception with the King! I couldn't go because we had two really heavy nights, one in Austria and then in Madrid. So, I hadn't slept a wink or eaten anything and we'd had a drink or two, so I was shattered. But that was a useful experience for what was to come. I reckon the first one was a bit of a beginner's performance! I never thought as a kid that I would play in a World Cup or win a European Championship. You don't think about stuff like that. You just focus on becoming a professional footballer, that might just happen, but not the rest."

Silva had a sensational Euro 2008 with Spain and though a flashpoint with Germany's Lukas Podolski ended his involvement in the final, a winner from Fernando Torres (above), ensured another major trophy

But it had happened and David Silva had been one of the stars of the tournament.

After a few weeks' rest, the 2008/09 campaign was soon upon the Canarian playmaker, but for the first time in his young career, he would be ruled out for several months with an ankle injury. It was bad enough to keep him out until December and restrict him to only 26 games, though he did help Valencia finish strongly and finish sixth in La Liga. The club, however, were in financial turmoil and reportedly 400 million euros in debt, resulting in a brief period where the players weren't paid their wages.

"I never thought as a kid that I would play in a World Cup or win a European Championship. You don't think about stuff like that"

Silva's final season with Valencia
came in 2009/10, at which point
the club's financial troubles had
other suitors around Europe on
alert for the Spaniard's signature

The whole campaign had proved to be a deflating one for David who was beginning to think about life away from the Mestalla.

He would remain for the 2009/10 season, wanting to feel settled in familiar surroundings ahead of the 2010 World Cup. Valencia had papered over the financial cracks with a loan and were still in desperate trouble. Prized assets Silva, Juan Mata and David Villa represented one avenue of quick revenue and all three again shone throughout a much-improved 2009/10 season with Valencia the best of the rest as Barcelona and Real Madrid battled it out for the La Liga title. By the end of the season, both David Silva and David Villa knew they would be playing their football elsewhere after the World Cup.

Silva clocked up 39 starts and recorded his best goal tally yet – 10 – while David Villa was in superb form, scoring 28 goals from 45 appearances, with Silva assisting many of them. It was the end of an era for both players and Villa would never quite enjoy such a productive campaign again.

"I was able to enjoy playing alongside him for many years at Valencia and for Spain," said Villa. "He's the kind of player that with the ball at his feet, a striker knows the killer pass could come at any second. And you have to be ready for it. He is a terrifying talent for a striker like me to have behind him. I think he's a lad who's got a mental toughness. He didn't get intimidated; he had a lot of character about him. And despite being so young, that character helped him take on a huge responsibility in a team like Valencia."

The World Cup was next on the agenda, but, understandably, David wanted to get his immediate future sorted before *La Roja* attempted to become world champions for the first time. One club, Manchester City, had been watching developments at the Mestalla very closely and Roberto Mancini, preparing for his first full season

as manager at City, was determined to build a team around David Silva.

Then Director of Football, Brian Marwood recalled: "We were in a period of quite a substantial amount of recruitment. We were made aware of some of the issues Valencia were facing in terms of their financial situation. We were made aware that some of their key players may well be available. David was one of those players."

David's agent, Amadeo Rengel, revealed that City were hell-bent on signing the Spain international and were in a position to make sure the deal went through. He said: "Mancini made it clear David was the right man for them, the same with Brian Marwood and CEO Garry Cook. In one of the conversations we had they made it clear that they wanted to sign David at any cost."

A productive 2009/10 campaign with Valencia saw Silva's goalscoring reach double figures for the first time, making him integral to Spain's 2010 World Cup chances as he joined up with the squad ahead of the tournament in South Africa

"I enjoyed six years at Valencia, they discovered me as a footballer and they will always be a special club. The time is right for me to seek a new challenge"

It was exactly what David wanted to hear. For him, it was all about who wanted him the most. It wasn't about money or instant success, he wanted to be part of something special, and City, rebuilding and shaping a squad with some of the most exciting talents in world football, were perfect.

On 30 June, 2010, City announced a deal had been agreed with Valencia to bring Silva to Manchester City. The fee was £24million and would be completed on 14 July, shortly after the World Cup had ended. At the time, David said: "I enjoyed six years at Valencia, they discovered me as a footballer and they will always be a special club for me. The time is right for me to seek a new challenge."

Deal agreed, there was now just the small matter of trying to help Spain win the one trophy the nation craved more than any other...

Silva basks in Spain's 2010 World Cup triumph, at which point he had agreed terms to join Manchester City the following season

# A new challenge

*(Un nuevo desafío)*

SIL V

# "I WANTED TO SIGN THIS GUY FIVE YEARS AGO FOR INTERNAZIONALE. HE HAS KEPT ME WAITING..."

**D**avid Silva had scored 21 goals in 119 La Liga appearances for Valencia, assisting 22 more, and became one of *Los Che's* prize assets at a time when the club was crippled by debt. Although both Barcelona and Real Madrid were keen to recruit him, Silva chose City as then-manager Roberto Mancini had been pursuing him for several months.

At the time, Chelsea were also keen to sign the gifted playmaker, so City, keen to tie up as many transfer deals as possible before the World Cup, moved quickly. However, the number of the potential targets Robert Mancini had identified meant concluding all deals before the tournament started wasn't going to be possible.

Jerome Boateng was secured on the eve of the South Africa tournament but Silva and Yaya Toure entered the competition as Valencia and Barcelona employees respectively. It was unusual, then, that Silva, not wanting any distractions before embarking on what would be a glorious journey with his country, decided to accept City's overtures while he was away with Spain.

David is unveiled at the Etihad ahead of the 2010/11 season, taking the No.21 shirt he favours for club and country

# "This was a club that was going places"

David agreed to join City as a Valencia player, but he arrived in Manchester as a World Cup winner. Spain defeated the Netherlands in the final in South Africa to claim a first ever world crown, though David started only one game – the opening group-stage loss to Switzerland – and appeared in the semi- final for four minutes. It mattered little – he had earned his World Cup medal and it was something nobody could ever take away from him. He had also watched his new team-mate Nigel de Jong somehow escape a red card from referee Howard Webb for a dangerously high tackle on Xabi Alonso.

"So much happened in a short space of time, my head was spinning," said Silva. "It was all a bit surreal and I hadn't really had chance to absorb what happened in South Africa. It was incredible and to sing and celebrate in front of more than one million people at our homecoming was something I'll remember forever. It was the best thing that could happen to any player. Unbelievable in fact."

When David arrived in Manchester a few days later, he had his World Cup medal in his back pocket (as you do) because he was worried he would lose it in transit. He was taken to the training ground, introduced to the players and then shown to the dressing room.

"They had put up a poster from the World Cup

David and his fellow Spanish World Cup winners arrive to a heroes' welcome in Madrid for a homecoming that City's new signing will always cherish

final," he recalled – but it wasn't the Spanish players lifting the trophy. He revealed: "It was Nigel de Jong's tackle on Xabi Alonso … that tackle."

Welcome to Manchester!

"I spent quite a lot of time with him," said Silva. "After the final I knew this was going to be a new team-mate of mine so I went looking for him, to say hard luck. As soon as I arrived in Manchester, he helped me settle in. I was like, 'as long as you save those tackles for the games and not training…!'

"I first got the news City were interested in signing me during my last matches with Valencia and I wanted to keep a clear mind until after the season finished. Then the World Cup was approaching so I had a good think so I could concentrate on the World Cup. Before I signed, I spoke to Fernando Torres and Pepe Reina about what it would be like moving to England and they confirmed it will be very competitive and that it is a great place to play. Money is not the main issue in England. What is important is trying to win trophies and playing in the Champions League. I knew I could do that here. This was a club that was going to places I wanted to visit.

An image of new club team-mate Nigel de Jong's high tackle on international team-mate Xabi Alonso during the 2010 World Cup final greeted David as he toured City's training facilities on his arrival in Manchester

"Things had been all over the place at Valencia. At one point, we weren't even getting paid. Construction on the new stadium stopped. The time had come where they had to sell. Mancini didn't have to do a big selling job, but what he did have to say was all very positive. City were the team who wanted me the most and went the extra mile. Other teams were interested, but Mancini got in contact a long time before the end of the season to see if I wanted

David shakes on his five-year City contract with CEO Ferran Soriano

"I enjoyed six years at Valencia, they discovered me as a footballer and they will always be a special club for me. But the time was right for me to seek a new challenge, and Manchester City was my new challenge. It turned out to be the best decision I've ever made in football"

to come here, and say I was a big part of his plans. When someone puts so much effort into demonstrating they want to sign you, you follow your heart.

"I can speak a bit of Italian, so we got by. He told me how ambitious everyone was. I was aware that City weren't in the top two or three English teams. I didn't go into the history too much, but I know they hadn't won a trophy for many, many years. But I was also made aware of their future plans, and the type of players they were buying to match the other clubs and try to win the title. I enjoyed six years at Valencia, they discovered me as a footballer and they will always be a special club for me. But the time was right for me to seek a new challenge, and Manchester City was my new challenge. It turned out to be the best decision I've ever made in football."

It was prophetic how David saw City's future – one laden with silverware. He foresaw a City side who not only would regularly challenge in Europe, but one that could potentially dominate at a domestic level. At the time, asked what his initial expectations were, he said: "A good first season for me would be to qualify for the Champions League – or to win a trophy, but my first target is to get into the team. Of course, I have to get to know my team-mates and then to fight for the league and the other competitions. I can't wait to play alongside Carlos Tevez, Emmanuel Adebayor, Yaya Toure and Nigel de Jong. There are so many great players here and I'm looking forward to playing alongside every one of them.

"Over the last few years, Manchester City's image has grown massively in Spain. The project here is getting more important with every year and with me it's very exciting that I'm now part of it. I think within two or three years it will be normal for City to be playing in the Champions League every year so I hope we can be on a par and challenge the best clubs around the world.

Of the players here I already know, Javi Garrido and I played in Spain's Under-21 side so we have a good relationship and have known each for a number of years. I called Javi to ask him about Manchester City and how things are here in Manchester and he told me I should get over here because this is a fantastic club.

"I want to learn the language as quickly as I can so I can communicate on a level playing field with everyone. I am looking forward to playing with my new team, but also I want to have a good rest because the last season and summer has been very long. I feel that everything is new but it's one of the reasons I'm looking forward to this season so much. It's a new challenge and I want to meet my team-mates and experience everything in what is a new life for me.

"I hope everything goes as well as my first visit to Manchester has because everybody has been very kind and helpful. I know that the weather in Manchester is different than Valencia or the Canaries – but I'm coming to Manchester to play football in a great team, not for sunbathing or going to the beach. I'm here to create and score goals and hopefully I can do both – but I'm looking forward the most to playing in front of our fans. I've heard that City supporters are loyal and passionate. They shout and sing all the time and they have always supported the team, even through difficult times. I am eager to experience that from inside the stadium and I'm excited by the challenge ahead for the team. I can't wait to get started."

After settling into training (right), Silva's first run-out for City came in the final 2010/11 pre-season friendly against former club Valencia, and he teased City fans with his skilful runs (above) during a 30-minute cameo

But some doubted whether his height and physicality could withstand the blood and thunder of the Premier League. English football is not for everyone and the climate has got the better of

# "I found it tough during those first few months. I was under a lot of pressure, having signed for a big fee I had no time off, so it was all a bit sudden"

many a foreign import over the years, particularly those used to all-year round sunshine and less imposing venues than – to use a well-worn cliché – a cold, wet night under the lights at Stoke.

Anyone who thought that about David, however, perhaps hadn't factored in his personality, his determination and work ethic. That year with Eibar had been invaluable. He could mix it with the best of them, and any opponent thinking they could push him around because of his size would soon be left looking a little foolish.

His father, Fernando, recalled: "The first year that he went to England, in the box where he signed his contract, there was a guy there from Malaga whose friends were City fans. They were saying that David was very small and doubted whether he would be a success at City and perhaps they'd made a mistake in signing him."

One thing he would need was time. Time to adjust, time to understand how the game was played in England and time to bed into his new team. He made his debut away to Spurs and it's fair to say that he struggled initially.

"Well, at the beginning it was a bit difficult," said David. "It was partly because I came straight from the World Cup, without having trained. Of course, I noticed straight away that it was very demanding physically and I needed to be right to play. So I found it tough during those first few months.

"You have to remember I was under a lot of pressure, having signed for a big fee I had no time off, so it was all a bit sudden. In

England, they play harder and faster and you have less time on the ball and less time to recover when you make a mistake."

He survived his debut away to Spurs, where despite being outplayed for long periods, a Joe Hart wonder show ensured City left White Hart Lane with a hard-earned 0-0 draw. David lasted the 90 minutes but looked exhausted at the end, reflected in a few uncharacteristic misplaced passes that left him shaking his head.

He was an unused substitute for the next game, a 3-0 home win over Liverpool, but started the UEFA Europa League second leg qualifier against Poli Timisoara a few days later when, on 59 minutes, he provided the first of many assists for Manchester City as his corner was nodded home by Dedryck Boyata during a 2-0 victory. He came on for the last 10 minutes or so of City's next game – a last-minute 1-0 defeat at Sunderland and again, he was a late sub in the next match at home to Blackburn Rovers with City again dropping points in a disappointing 1-1 draw. Mancini had initially played Silva as a left winger – but against Red Bull Salzburg in the Europa League just a few days later, he switched the Spain star to his more favoured central attacking midfield position and it immediately paid dividends.

David's City debut came in the goalless draw at Spurs (left) as the 2010/11 season got under way, and the following month he was celebrating his first goal for the Club (above) during a 2-0 Europa League win over Red Bull Salzburg, the same team he had opening his Valencia goalscoring account against four years earlier

With just eight minutes played, Silva drilled home a low shot from just inside the box to score his first goal for the Club and, just before the break, was denied a second by a fine save by the Austrian's keeper. Even so early in his City career, Silva looked liberated and glided around the pitch effortlessly throughout the game until his 83rd-minute substitution. He'd shown glimpses of the future, played with a smile on his face and was finally off and running.

# The boy who made history

*El chico que hizo historia*

# "I'M FEELING GOOD IN MYSELF NOW AND WITH TIME ON THE PITCH, I THINK ALL THE PIECES WILL COME TOGETHER"

In the grand scheme of things, David Silva's bedding in period at City was fairly brief. He was finding his feet quickly and already proving the doubters wrong. Roberto Mancini's side had a bit of everything – experience, steely determination, an abundance of ability, creative flair and belief – belief that they had come together to make history.

From back to front there was world-class quality. In defence there was England's no.1 Joe Hart, with Vincent Kompany, Joleon Lescott, Kolo Toure and Pablo Zabaleta in front of him. In midfield, there was the Dutch enforcer Nigel de Jong, with English grit and work ethic in the shape of James Milner and Gareth Barry. Add to that the Ivorian powerhouse that was Yaya Toure – who was beginning to show just what a wise capture he had been from Barcelona in the summer – and the inimitable Carlos Tevez leading the line. Silva was the creator-in-chief – the playmaker that knitted everything together and dictated the tempo like a conductor guiding his orchestra. There was a way to go yet and like any new machinery,

there would be snags along the way and a few bolts would need to be tightened. The odd part might even need changing, but there was something special about this group of players.

The first hint that the side assembled partly by Mark Hughes – and upgraded by Mancini – was capable of genuinely challenging for silverware was the 1-0 win over Carlo Ancelotti's Chelsea at the Etihad in September 2010. Chelsea arrived with a 100 per cent record, but Tevez's 59th-minute goal proved to be the only goal of the game and moved City up to fourth in the Premier League. A limping Silva left the pitch to a warm reception on 77 minutes, but thankfully, it was a minor issue and nothing serious. But if there had been only flashes of Silva's potential by the time City travelled to the west coast to take on Blackpool at Bloomfield Road, it was his name that was on the lips of more than 6,000 travelling fans from Manchester on a blustery afternoon by the seaside.

If anyone had still been unsure about David Silva going into that game, his 25-minute cameo against Ian Holloway's side banished any doubts in one fell swoop and the start of a decade of magic began in earnest. It was three months since he had won the World Cup with Spain, the fatigue of a long summer was finally out of his legs, he was understanding how his team-mates played and

Silva fires home his first Premier League goal for City, in a 3-2 mid-October win at Blackpool, and mesmerising onlookers after his 66th-minute introduction

Silva admits his first few weeks at City were tiring as he adapted to the intensity of English football so soon after his World Cup exertions with Spain

where his role was in the side and he was mentally refreshed. He was ready.

At the time, he said: "I was slightly tired from the World Cup. I was physically and mentally drained, too. So the first few weeks were difficult. Moving to England was tough to start off with, it was difficult physically, the speed of the game was different and I had to adapt to a different lifestyle. The language was a problem, even when playing, but things have gone very well for me since. The weather's gone a lot colder, but I don't mind because everything else is going so well for me.

"I've adapted very quickly and now I feel at home, very happy and I think it's now showing through in my football. Everything has been made so much easier by the way I've been treated so well by my team-mates and everyone here at the Club who has given me a helping hand.

Our new No.21 makes his first competitive home appearance for City in the Europa League qualifying win over Poli Timisoara

City strikers like Edin Dzeko were soon the
beneficiaries of Silva's vision and excellent link-up
play as the Spaniard settled into life at the Club

"I think I am getting
up to speed now.
I want to do my bit
for the team so we
can all achieve our
goals together"

"I think that, physically, I'm feeling better day by day. Of course, I need to get a few more minutes on the pitch to get to optimum fitness levels and I'm sure that will happen with so many games coming up. I've been away a couple of times with the national team, and that hasn't helped. When I first arrived at City, I hadn't played for a while and my body felt tired, but I'm feeling good in myself now, and with time on the pitch, I think all the pieces will come together.

"I've settled well in Manchester, but again, the international break probably came at a bad time for me. I love the Club and fans already and I'm starting to learn English so I can communicate better with my team-mates, so as time goes on, things will get easier for me. I've been treated really well by everyone and the other players have been great, but I need to push on now. The Premier League is exactly the way I thought it would be with a high tempo to the games. It's very competitive and a challenge, but one I'm enjoying and ultimately hope to thrive in.

"I think I'm getting up to speed now. It's not just about playing games, it's about getting more training sessions under your belt – something I've been able to do more of late – I'm getting there, just more slowly than I would have liked! We have a great squad and it takes time for all the new players to adapt and gel together. I've been playing more on the right side and having the freedom to play and search for the spaces is good for my football. It is always good to play. I think that things are starting to work for me. I want to do my bit for the team and continue to be successful so we can all achieve our goals together. I think we will become stronger as a team as the season progresses – we just need to ensure we keep within touching distance of the top. I think we'll have a very good season."

Silva started on the bench against Blackpool, who were more

than punching above their weight in mid-table and could even have moved within one point of City with a victory. Indeed, with 65 minutes played, the contest was very much in the balance. But Mancini decided it was time to bring Silva on and Emmanuel Adebayor was the man he hauled off. Within two minutes, City were ahead as Silva's low cross was turned home by Tevez. The goal put City 1-0 up and sparked a frantic last third of the game, with the hosts levelling on 78, Tevez restoring the lead and both sides going close to scoring again. But on 90 minutes, the three points were sealed with the goal that showed Silva's brilliance as he picked up a short free-kick on the right of the Blackpool box, jinked past one challenge, cut inside of another and then curled a superb shot past the keeper from 10 yards to make it 3-1. He ripped his shirt off, waved it around and – despite being mobbed by his team-mates – managed to get to the legions of travelling fans along one side of Bloomfield Road to celebrate with them

It had begun.

City won the game 3-2, but everything would be different from that day forward.

Silva makes his introduction at Bloomfield Road (above) and within minutes turns the game in City's favour, first setting up our opener then scoring what proved to be the winner (right)

While the Premier League would prove just out of reach for Mancini's side, Champions League football for the first time seemed likely. Despite topping the table in mid-February after a 4-3 win over Wolves, just five wins in the next 12 meant targets had to be realigned and ambition tempered. At least for the time being. The Europa League run had ended at the Round of 16 stage, meaning

Silva's debut season with
the Blues saw him lift the
FA Cup — City's first piece
of silverware in 35 years

that the only possible silverware City could win was the FA Cup – something the Club hadn't done since 1969, some 42 years before. Both Leicester City and Notts County had been dispatched after replays and David scored the third goal in a 3-0 victory over Aston Villa to put the Blues in the quarter-final. Victory over Reading then set up a Manchester derby at Wembley Stadium and a chance for City to put down a real marker against Sir Alex Ferguson's side, who were closing in on another Premier League title.

The FA Cup semi-final turned out to be an unforgettable occasion, with City fans fantastic throughout and Yaya Toure's 52-minute goal enough to settle the contest. In many ways, it was a changing of the guard. It was City's turn to be the dominant force in the city and though there were no trophies in the Etihad cabinet just yet, it seemed only a matter of time. Before the FA Cup final, City had to secure Champions League football and this was achieved with a 1-0 victory over Spurs and ensured the season was a success, no matter what happened against Stoke in the final.

But a generation of City fans had never seen the Club win a trophy and the opportunity to end a 35-year wait for silverware against a Stoke side who had been battling against relegation for much of the campaign, was too good to let slip. The tension on the day was palpable – almost unbearable for the 30,000 or so hope-filled Mancunians.

David, as he had been doing on and off throughout the campaign, started on the right wing, often cutting inside to try and find the opening. He came agonisingly close to breaking the deadlock just before half-time as Mario Balotelli's attempt was saved, but he hit the loose ball into the ground and over the crossbar. As time went on, it seemed one goal for either side would settle the game, and it proved true with Silva at the heart of the move that resulted in the winner.

"Once you win, you get used to winning, and that's not a bad thing. The FA Cup was a real highlight and an important milestone for the Club"

Racing into the box onto Balotelli's back-heel, he was first to the ball and returned the pass to the Italian striker – he saw his shot blocked but only as far as Yaya Toure who emphatically drove the ball home from eight yards to spark scenes of wild celebrations. At the final whistle, there were emotional scenes at Wembley Stadium. The wait was over and on the big screen, a counter reversed from 35 years to zero (mimicking a flag the United fans had updated each season) to joyous applause.

He would be the last person to claim it was his influence that had made the 2010/11 season – his first in English football – the

fantastic success it had been, but David Silva had played a big part. A first trophy for 35 years and Champions League football secured via a third-place finish in the Premier League.

"That was the turning point for success," said David. "Once you win, you get used to winning, and that's not a bad thing. The same has happened in the Spanish national team – winning the first title was a game-changer and we carried on winning. So the FA Cup was a real highlight and an important milestone for the Club."

Indeed it was. But there was much more to come from Manchester City and David Silva in particular…

# SILVA
## MEMORIES
### 2010/11

102

# The
*(El Mago)*

# Magician

# "IF HE HAD GONE TO BARÇA TWO YEARS AGO, EVERYONE WOULD SAY HE'S ONE OF THE BEST PLAYERS IN THE WORLD – AND HE IS ONE OF THE BEST PLAYERS IN THE WORLD"

One trophy in the bag and the wait for silverware over, City's next target was the Premier League title. It had been 42 years since City had last been crowned champions of England, but with a few more summer additions – most notably Sergio Aguero and Samir Nasri – there was a feeling around the Club that winning the league was more than a distinct possibility.

The opening game of the season saw David Silva sparkle in what looked a more central, freer role, and the introduction of Aguero from the bench saw the Argentinian score twice and set another up for Silva in a 4-0 victory over Swansea City. There seemed to be an immediate understanding between Aguero and Silva, clearly operating on the same wavelength, and it was definite cause for optimism.

And David, now adding goals to his sizeable repertoire, scored again in the next match – a 3-2 win away to Bolton Wanderers – with a wicked left-foot shot from 20 yards completely fooling

There was an instant connection between Silva and summer signing Sergio Aguero, and these scenes of celebration would become a common sight

# 'Stop Silva, stop City'

keeper Jussi Jaaskelainen to put City ahead. And if any evidence of how settled he now was in the team had been needed, the 5-1 victory away to Spurs underlined what a player the Blues had on their hands. Silva gave a mesmeric performance in a game that was a wake-up call for the rest of the Premier League. This City team were the real deal.

David's vision was giving City something extra, and his understanding with Sergio Aguero was evolving game by game. He assisted the Argentinian twice more in the 3-0 win over Wigan Athletic and then in the 2-2 draw with Fulham. And while it was a little early to suggest 'stop Silva, stop City', that's exactly what Everton tried to do in game six of the 2011/12 season. Bear in mind he had barely been a City player for more than a year, but the BBC Sport report of the game against the Toffees illustrates just how quickly his profile was rising in the Premier League.

Phil McNulty wrote: "David Moyes had clearly earmarked Silva as central to City's threat and he deployed youngster Jack Rodwell to man-mark the Spaniard. And when he received a yellow card for a foul on Silva, responsibility briefly switched to Phil Neville, until he drew similar punishment from referee Webb after a clash with Silva.

David evades the close attention of Jack Rodwell as Everton deploy man-markers on our slaloming Spaniard, but to little effect

"Silva, who hit the woodwork and saw a

goal disallowed, was at his creative best as City wrapped up the win with just a minute left. Everton substitute Royston Drenthe lost possession in midfield and Silva threaded through a perfect invitation for Milner to slide his finish past Tim Howard."

September's efforts earned David his first Premier League Player of the Month award as well as City's fan-voted Player of the Month accolade.

But he was just getting started. Four-goal salvos against both Blackburn and Aston Villa meant City travelled to Old Trafford to take on Manchester United in pole position in the Premier League It was a chance for City to further prove they were more than a match for the Reds and serious title challengers and – inspired by a mesmeric performance by Silva – it turned out to be United's biggest home defeat for 55 years, with David at the heart of everything, assisting two goals and scoring one himself.

Edin Dzeko was the beneficiary of more pinpoint accuracy from Silva, the Bosnian wrapping up a 6-1 win at Old Trafford by stroking home a sumptuous through-ball just two minutes after our No.21 got on the scoresheet himself (right)

But it had been his sumptuous through-ball to Edin Dzeko for the final goal of the 6-1 rout – that will live long in the memory of City fans as he controlled a headed clearance just inside his own half and then span and volleyed an inch-perfect through-pass that Dzeko didn't even have to adjust his run for and the Bosnian made no mistake from the edge of the box.

Again, the BBC waxed lyrical about David's performance, with Phil McNulty writing: "And with some United supporters actually pleading with referee Clattenburg to put them out of their misery, one more moment of brilliance from the magical Silva found Dzeko surging into the area to finish left-footed for his second."

Roberto Mancini spoke for every City fan when asked about Silva: "We're lucky to have him here, he is one of the best players in the world"

"I don't know if this is the best I have ever played in my career, but it is very close. I feel calm, happy and motivated and I think that is showing in my football"

Two more victories followed over QPR and Wolves before an unbeaten Newcastle United arrived at the Etihad. David spoke before the game, saying: "It will be a difficult game. We are at home and hopefully we'll play as well as we have done in our previous home games and will get the three points. We'll play our way and they will play theirs – we hope that our way is better and we win!

"Of course, for me it's the same. I always play the same way and try my hardest for both City and Spain, and so far things are going well so I hope it carries on like this until the end of the league. I am getting better at scoring goals, but I would like to be better at heading and defending, if possible.

"I don't know if this is the best I have ever played in my career, but it is very close. I feel calm, happy and motivated and I think that is showing in my football. I am happy because things are going very well and I feel very comfortable in the team and in Manchester.

"On the pitch, there are no fixed positions. We can move in attack freely, following the coaches' instructions. We have trained this way and we all practise being playmakers and creating chances. We work hard and have a licence to be creative in everything we do. As for my own role, I have to see where other players are and I try to fill the free space – and it is the same for the others and so far, it has proved to be very effective."

Under Roberto Mancini, David was able to express himself and flourish in the Premier League and the Italian was in no doubt that City's gain was La Liga's loss.

"Silva is a top, top player," he said. "I don't know why he didn't go to Barça or Real Madrid because he's Spanish and a Spain international, but we are lucky because he's here. If he had gone to Barça two years ago, everyone would say he's one of the best players in the world – and he is one of the best players in the world. He's different from Lionel Messi and Cristiano Ronaldo because they are strikers and score a lot of goals. but I think he's on the same level as Xavi and Andrés Iniesta." High praise indeed.

Back on the pitch and City seemed to be steamrollering towards the Premier League title, and a 2-0 win against Bolton Wanderers at the start of March saw the Blues pull five points clear of United. There were just 11 games remaining and still plenty of hard work ahead, but United had the advantage of being in this position many times before and that experience would soon start to have a bearing on the title race.

City couldn't have timed a blip any worse than the spring dip that was about to follow, starting with a 1-0 defeat away to Swansea. The response was impressive, particularly as United had gone from five points adrift after the Bolton result to four points in front ahead of City's midweek win against Chelsea. In that game, City fell behind with an hour played, but goals from Sergio Aguero and a returning from exile Carlos Tevez assisted winner for Samir Nasri kept the Blues on track.

The mid-March victory over Chelsea (above) helped close the gap on United at the summit, but a return of just two points from the next three games left City with another huge task in our bid to land a first Premier League title

But Mancini's men handed back the initiative to United by first drawing 1-1 away to Stoke and then 3-3 at home to Sunderland – despite having been 3-1 down with 85 minutes on the clock. Four points dropped in two games and United's win over Blackburn a few days later put the Reds five points clear with seven games remaining. But it was about to get worse, as a late Mikel Arteta goal saw City lose at Arsenal and, as a result, United pulled eight points clear with six games remaining. Just 11 points from their remaining half-dozen matches and they would have the ultimate last laugh for the 6-1 drubbing they'd been subjected to earlier in the campaign.

Silva's dinked effort sails over Ben Foster and into the West Brom goal, cementing a stylish 4-0 victory over the Baggies and re-energising City's title bid

'With three games remaining, City knew that a win over United and then victory against Newcastle and QPR would bring the Premier League title back to the Etihad Stadium. It was incredible drama'

It seemed like mission impossible, but City had to keep believing. And that belief shone through in the game that followed. Inspired by a sparkling David Silva performance, the Spaniard capped a starring role with a delightful chip that completed a 4-0 win over West Brom. With the news that lowly Wigan Athletic had recorded a shock 1-0 win over United that same night, suddenly it was a five-point gap and not eight – and United still had to come to the Etihad Stadium.

Reinvigorated, City then went to Carrow Road and thrashed Norwich 6-1, and though United won their game, the weekend after would see everything change. United played Everton ahead of City's game away to Wolves and watching City fans could hardly believe what they were seeing as United threw a 4-2 lead away in the closing minutes to draw 4-4 with Everton at Old Trafford. If Mancini's side needed a shot in the arm, the Toffees had provided it and the 2-0 win at Molineux that followed set up arguably the most important Manchester derby of all time.

With three games remaining, City knew that a win over United and then victory against Newcastle and QPR would bring the Premier League title back to the Etihad Stadium. It was incredible drama and an almost unthinkable scenario just four games earlier when City had trailed the Reds by eight points. Of course, in a tense and almost unbearable Manchester derby, it was Silva who provided the assist for Vincent Kompany's winner on half-time, and suddenly, it was on. Win the final two games and the title was City's.

"We knew we had to win," said Silva after the game. "Mentally we were ready to win it. We did that and now we have to continue concentrating on the job. If we end up winning the title, Monday's win could be the most important win of my club career. But we have to win the championship for that win to mean something.

Silva helps keep Newcastle at arm's length in a 2-0 win that put Mancini's men in reach of the league crown

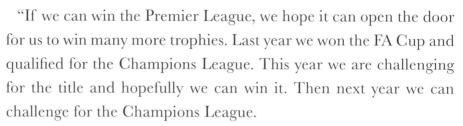

"If we can win the Premier League, we hope it can open the door for us to win many more trophies. Last year we won the FA Cup and qualified for the Champions League. This year we are challenging for the title and hopefully we can win it. Then next year we can challenge for the Champions League.

"Beating United has given us the confidence we need for the last two games. It has been a very long and tough season. The Newcastle game is like a final for us now. We have to win it. I am surprised that United have given up an eight-point lead, but don't forget we had a massive lead as well and lost it. It has been a very competitive season. In the dressing room after the game you could see the boss was delighted. He told us that we all had played a great match. But he also reminded us that we must concentrate on next Sunday.

"I have been quite unlucky in the second half of the season because not only have I had constant knocks on the same ankle that has caused me a lot of trouble in the past, but just at the moment when we had a dip in form as a team. I'm having a lot of treatment to get movement in my ankle. It is feeling slightly better, but it helps that the team are playing better. All I'm thinking about is the next match on Sunday – we have to go to Newcastle and win."

And win City did, with Yaya Toure scoring both second-half goals in a 2-0 win to leave the Blues needing to beat relegation-threatened QPR to take the title. What happened in that game is still the stuff of nightmares and, ultimately, the wildest dreams imaginable. It began as per script, with Pablo Zabaleta giving City the lead just before the break, but QPR struck twice after the restart to lead 2-1 with 66 minutes played. Could it transpire that all the hard work to get back in pole position would all be undone on the final day? As the board went up for an additional five minutes and City were still 2-1 down, it seemed it might. United were 2-0 up at

Sunderland and, in the live Premier League table, were three points clear with just a few minutes of the 2011/12 campaign remaining.

A corner a couple of minutes into added time from Silva found the head of Edin Dzeko to make it 2-2 and, a couple of minutes later, Aguero exchanged passes with Mario Balotelli on the edge of the box before drifting past one challenge and drilling a low shot past QPR keeper Paddy Kenny.

City were champions.

It was incredible, but it had happened and the Blues were finally the Premier League champions. It's fair to say both the players and supporters were in a mild state of shock and after the trophy lift and wild celebrations that followed, David was interviewed on the Etihad pitch about what had just happened. He said: "We made the game very hard for ourselves, but we kept battling to the end. We were in control early on and then I thought it was going to be very tough – but in the end, we managed to do it. I'm happy for everything. For everyone here because we've won a big trophy like the Premier League. For my family, too, and I hope all the fans will enjoy the victory like I will. Like I said, I'm really happy. This team is just getting better and better and let's hope next season we can be even better."

It had been a remarkable season for Manchester City and a wonderful second season for David Silva. It was no coincidence City had ended the decades wait for silverware after he had arrived and now the FA Cup and Premier League had been secured in his first two seasons at the Club.

His 49 appearances had yielded 19 assists and eight goals in all competitions and his team-mates recognised that sizeable contribution as he was voted the Manchester City Players' Player of the Year and he also won the wider respect of his peers as he was also voted into the prestigious PFA Premier League Team of the Year.

An unforgettable year for the boy from Arguineguin…

Silva enjoys the title celebrations with his team-mates after a dramatic and triumphant end to a memorable campaign with City. Next up, the European Championships and the defence of Spain's title...

SILVA
MEMORIES
2011/12

123

# Home is where the heart is

*El hogar está donde está el corazón*

Another international tournament, another trophy for Spain's Silva, who was one of the stand-out performers at Euro 2012

# "BEING HERE REALLY DOES FEEL JUST LIKE HOME FOR ME"

**B**arely six weeks after lifting the Premier League trophy with City, David Silva was celebrating a third major title with Spain in four years as *La Roja* successfully defended their Euro 2008 success by taking the Euro 2012 crown in Kyiv. David carried his club form into the national team, played in all six games, scored twice and earned his place in the UEFA Team of the Tournament.

Andres Iniesta, regarded as one of the greatest Spain players of all time, was under no illusion how important David was to the team. "He pulls the strings on the pitch," he said. "He is just a brilliant footballer with great movement and he can score, assist or whatever. He is a player who decides a game. He gave the national team that wide range of options on the pitch."

Iniesta's former Barcelona team-mate Xavi concurred with those sentiments as he added: "He's a spectacular footballer. Right from when he played for Eibar and Celta and when he went back to Valencia. For the national team he has been a cornerstone of that generation of highly talented Spanish footballers, that went on to win the European Championship, the World Cup and then the second European title. David was a vital component and absolutely essential to that team."

Spain had a supremely talented group of players who had grown together at various youth and club levels and made the most of their talent.

Silva believes it might never happen again that one country wins back-to-back Euros with a World Cup squeezed in the middle. "It was a cycle that will be remembered throughout history," he said, "because winning three trophies on the bounce – Euro 2008, the World Cup and another Euro in 2012 – will be very difficult to repeat."

It's safe to say that David's performances for Spain had La Liga giants Barcelona and Real Madrid casting envious eyes at one of City's prized assets. But David wasn't interested in either of them and whether they enquired (which is likely) or not, he was keen to commit himself to his life in Manchester and the Club were desperate to ensure he wasn't going anywhere.

The reigning Premier League champions had already secured the long-term futures of Joe Hart and Vincent Kompany, so it was only logical to offer David a new, lengthy contract extension to ensure he remained at the Etihad. The renegotiation was uncomplicated and

David returns to City training as a double European Championship winner, having played an instrumental role in Spain's Euro 2012 triumph

Silva's new City deal
would seal his services
for another five years

agreed quickly and just a few weeks into the 2012/13 campaign it was announced that David had penned a new deal that would keep him at City until 2017. It was news that was lapped up by City fans who had taken the diminutive Gran Canarian to their hearts.

After the deal was announced, David said: "I'm very pleased because I've been here for two years now and I feel very happy here at the Club, in the city and with all the people. So now I'm delighted to be extending my contract and being here really does feel just like home for me. We've won the Premier League title and two other trophies too (the FA Community Shield had been secured in August), and the team is growing. We are now aiming at

There were mixed fortunes for Silva and City as the 2012/13 campaign got under way; having made a solid start to our Premier League defence, remaining unbeaten until December's derby, the Blues were unable to prolong our European adventure after coming up against tough opposition in the Champions League group stage

"These last two years have gone very well and so let's hope that the next five go as well or even better"

the Champions League and so that also is another reason to want to stay here and try and win it. As I said, I feel very comfortable here and I want to try and win trophies like those.

"These last two years have gone very well and so let's hope that the next five go as well or even better. The fans have always given me their support since I arrived here, and recently they have been wanting me to sign, so hopefully this goes some way to thanking them for the affection they've shown towards me, something which also helped me decide to put pen to paper."

City began their defence of their Premier League crown well, though the new signings brought in during the summer lacked the sparkle of the previous two years' additions, with Javi Garcia, Maicon, Scott Sinclair, Jack Rodwell and Matija Nastasic ultimately all going on to have disappointing spells with the Blues. There was no title hangover as such, though one wonders how the season might have gone had City held on to the 2-1 lead at the Bernabeu against Real Madrid in the opening Champions League group-stage match. Real scored twice in the last four minutes to win the game 3-2, and Mancini's side would fail to win any of their six group games, exiting the competition and failing to even make the cut for the Europa League after failing to secure third spot.

Already out of the League Cup by September, City's focus was now on retaining the title and having a tilt at the FA Cup, and after remaining unbeaten for the opening 15 Premier League games, the Blues went into the Manchester derby knowing victory would put them top of the table over United – but a last-minute winner saw United leave the Etihad with a 3-2 win and instead go six points clear at the top.

David was doing his best, as were the rest of the team, but there was a touch of stardust missing from the campaign. Perhaps the emotionally exhausting end to the previous season, plus the Euros was taking its toll? City's response was good, winning eight of the next nine games in all competitions including a 2-0 win over Fulham in mid-January in which Silva bagged his first City brace.

Afterwards, assistant manager David Platt said: "David Silva had a great time last season and his recent performances have been very good. He does great things for us, but he has missed the goals his performances deserve. He got two today and should have had three."

Something still wasn't quite right and maybe the pressure of trying to win back-to-back titles and United's determination to claim back the city bragging rights in Sir Alex Ferguson's last season were also playing their part. The next three games would see the tiny cracks that were appearing widen, with the champions taking just two points from a possible nine, including a lacklustre 3-1 defeat at Southampton that all-but ended any lingering hopes of overhauling United who would move 12 points clear with 12 games remaining the following day.

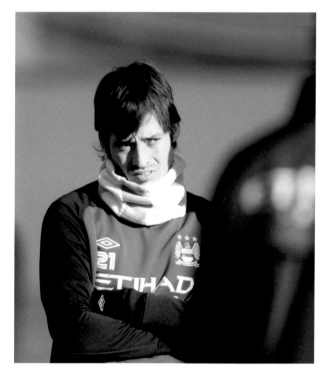

Despite Silva's first City brace in the win over Fulham (right), hopes of retaining the Premier League title started to slip away from the Blues as they entered February

The FA Cup became the only hope of ending the campaign with any major silverware and City bounced back immediately with a 4-0 win over Leeds United to book a quarter-final tie with Championship side Barnsley.

Silva summed up the mood at the time as he previewed the tie: "This is another chance to get to Wembley and it is very important that we win this game. The league is very, very difficult now. But we can reach the FA Cup final, so we have to focus on

**Silva's 2012/13 season heads towards a disappointing conclusion as City lose the FA Cup final to spirited underdogs Wigan at Wembley**

# "Wembley is an amazing place to play football and I have been lucky enough to have already played there. Now I want to get to another final"

this game. We are now only one game away from going back to Wembley again and on paper we should beat Barnsley, but they are in the quarter-final because they deserve to be, so we will have to be very cautious and try to win the game.

"Wembley is an amazing place to play football and I have been lucky enough to have already played there. Now I want to get to another final. In Spain, it is much more difficult for the smaller teams to rise to the top, but we have seen that in England smaller teams can get to the finals, such as Bradford City in the Capital One Cup. The nearest I came to be playing in a giant-killing game was when I was at Valencia. We weren't a big team, but we won the cup and beat Barcelona, who were the biggest team in Spain – it's not quite the same but it still was something of a shock at the time."

Silva scored in a 5-0 win that booked a semi-final spot with Chelsea at Wembley, and in the league, five wins out of the next six – including a 2-1 win away to United – kept title hopes alive, though highly unlikely – but those were finally extinguished by Spurs who triumphed 3-1 at White Hart Lane to leave United needing one win from their last six matches to reclaim the Premier League crown. City saw off Chelsea to book a final date

with Wigan Athletic at Wembley, but even that ended with huge disappointment as overwhelming favourites City lost to about-to-be-relegated Wigan Athletic in one of the biggest FA Cup final upsets for decades.

It would be Mancini's last game in charge as he was dismissed shortly after and Brian Kidd took the role as caretaker for the final two games of the season. None of the City players – even David Silva – had been able to turn a reasonable season into a great season. The fact was City still finished runners-up in the Premier League and had reached the FA Cup final, and on paper, many clubs would be very happy with that – probably 90 in the Football League family – but it just felt as if the team had somehow taken a backwards step, and the failure to progress in the Champions League had also been a cause for concern.

The end-of-season anguish felt after the FA Cup final defeat meant Silva and City would need to come back stronger for the 2013/14 campaign

David's five goals and 11 assists were well down on his previous season's stats and the same could be said of almost every member of the first-team squad. Title hangover, emotional exhaustion or perhaps Mancini had simply taken the team as far as he could and a new voice was needed to lead what was still a very talented group of footballers. Whoever took on the role, they would need to quickly identify that having a fresh, rested and firing on all cylinders David Silva was crucial to attempting to wrestle the Premier League title back from United in 2013/14...

# SILVA
## MEMORIES
### 2012/13

140

# Licence to thrill

*Licencia para emocionar*

#mcfc

# "IN THE BACK OF OUR MINDS, WE REMEMBERED 2012 AND WINNING IT IN THE LAST MINUTE, SO THAT KEPT US GOING..."

**N**ew City boss Manuel Pellegrini was announced during the summer of 2013 and the Chilean promised to play attacking football and put the smiles back on everyone's faces again after a flat end to the previous campaign.

Pellegrini was a huge admirer of David Silva from his days as Villarreal and Real Madrid boss when he frequently starred against his teams.

He had moved from the Bernabeu to manage Malaga in 2010 and one of his early purchases included a player who had been lined up to replace Silva at Valencia – Francisco Roman Alarcon Suarez – better known simply as Isco.

A precocious attacking midfield talent, Pellegrini attempted to bring him to City and be one of his first major signings, but the 21-year-old was instead snapped up by Real Madrid. Pellegrini had, it seemed, envisaged a midfield that included Silva and Isco, but he was happy to have at least one of them in his number at City.

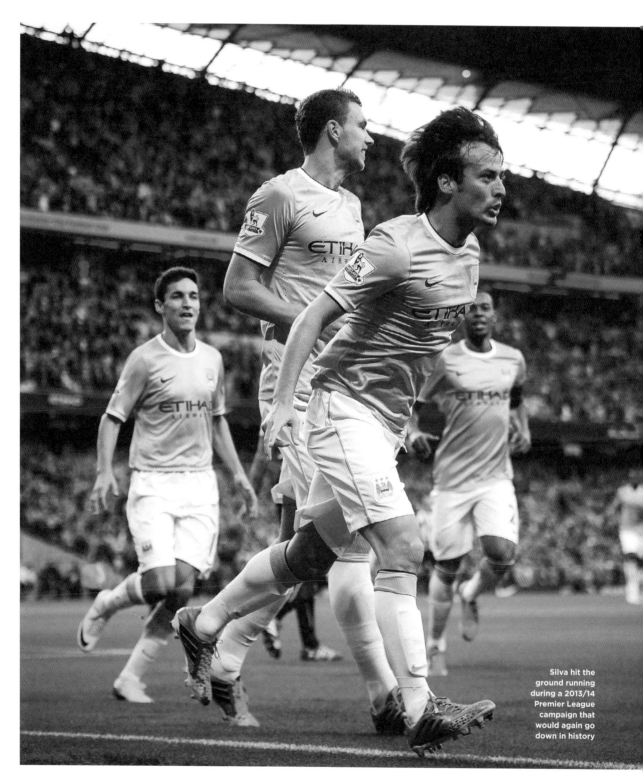

Silva hit the
ground running
during a 2013/14
Premier League
campaign that
would again go
down in history

# 'The best team on the planet'

Pellegrini would hand Silva the licence to roam and create his magic in a freer role than the one he'd had under Roberto Mancini. To achieve this, the wily new City boss purchased Shakhtar Donetsk holding midfielder Fernandinho, as well as adding trusted La Liga talent in the shape of striker Alvaro Negredo and winger Jesus Navas.

City's opening game of the 2013/14 campaign, at home to Newcastle, couldn't have gone much better. Silva, clearly playing in a more advanced role, met Edin Dzeko's cross to head home with just six minutes on the clock as the Blues went on to win 4-0, playing some sparkling stuff. It suggested City might be back on track in double-quick time, but the opening weeks would prove anything but smooth for the new manager.

A surprise 3-2 defeat to Cardiff City the week after and a nervy 2-0 victory over Hull City was followed with a dull 0-0 draw away to Stoke. There were clearly teething problems for Pellegrini to solve and losing Silva for the next month to injury didn't help matters, either. City blew hot (beating United 4-1) and cold (losing 3-2 to Aston Villa) in Silva's absence and though he returned at the start of October, Pep Guardiola's Bayern Munich destroyed City at the Etihad with a chastening 3-1 victory that could have been many more.

Silva helped get life under Manuel Pellegrini off to a flying start by opening City's goalscoring account just six minutes into the 2013/14 Premier League campaign

By the time City lost 1-0 to Sunderland in early November, Pellegrini had lost Silva for a month with a calf injury and the Blues had fallen to eighth in the table. The early optimism had been replaced by concern with four defeats and just six wins from the first 11 games. But then, everything seemed to fall into place and a mis-firing City became a mesmeric City, winning 18 of the next 20 games in all competitions and establishing themselves as contenders on four fronts and scoring 69 goals in the process at an average of 3.5 per game.

After the 5-1 thrashing of Tottenham, with Silva running amok during a breathtaking performance at White Hart Lane, City moved to the top of the Premier League. Spurs boss Tim Sherwood said: "They are the best team on the planet, certainly the best team in the Premier League. We've played the champions today. It was difficult with level numbers, but once we were down to 10 it was over as a spectacle."

BBC *Match of the Day* pundit Alan Hansen added: "Tottenham were playing against possibly the best team in the world, with some of the greatest players in the world. They have gone away from home against a team who have taken 16 points from 18, and are going for the top four, and dismissed them with consummate ease. In the first half-hour they could have had five – their fluency, passing and movement was just mesmeric."

David's injury-sustained absence in September meant Pellegrini had to rethink his creative options during a topsy-turvy run of form for City, but the Spaniard's return provided a shot in the arm to our title hopes towards the end of November

Just how far could this Pellegrini and Silva-inspired City go? Poor luck in the Champions League Round of 16 saw City paired with Barcelona, who would edge both legs, and the 1-0 home loss to Chelsea in the Premier League, goalless draw away to Norwich and the surprise FA Cup quarter-final exit to Wigan had been offset by

'The Capital One Cup triumph at Wembley gave David his fourth winner's medal in just four years – but the medal he and the rest of his team-mates craved was the one awarded for another Premier League title'

a 3-1 Capital One Cup triumph against Sunderland at Wembley. That gave David his fourth winner's medal in just four years – a more than acceptable return – but the medal he and the rest of his team-mates craved more than any other was the one awarded for securing another Premier League title.

City and Liverpool were emerging main contenders to leaders Chelsea, and a trip to the KC Communications Stadium to face Hull looked winnable on paper, but when Vincent Kompany was sent off just 10 minutes in, the game suddenly looked in doubt. However, from the moment the Belgian left the pitch until the final whistle, David Silva stepped up to lead the team to victory. Just four minutes after the dismissal, Silva cut in from the right before curling a 25-yard left-foot shot into the top corner to give the Blues belief and some breathing space. In a tense battle, Edin Dzeko sealed victory on 90 minutes and the emotional scenes between Joe Hart, the travelling City fans and the rest of the team on the final whistle suggested this had been a pivotal victory. Silva had been at his magical best, but those fighting qualities and will to win had perhaps never been more evident. There was still hard work ahead, but there seemed to be real momentum behind City again.

Silva had the bit between his teeth and was at his magical best in the 5-0 win over Fulham at the Etihad and the 3-0 win over Manchester United at Old Trafford where he struck the post in the first few seconds with Edin Dzeko putting home the rebound as he gave another masterful performance. His goal away to Arsenal in the next game was not enough to earn three points as the Gunners took a point in the 1-1 draw at the Emirates, leaving just two points between Chelsea, Liverpool and City at the top of the table, and though the Blues eased past Southampton in the next game, there was to be a sizeable double hiccup that put Liverpool very much in the driving seat for the Premier League crown.

What was billed as potentially the title decider at Anfield was up next, and City couldn't have started much worse, going 2-0 down with just 26 minutes played. Victory would leave Liverpool needing just four more wins to become champions, but David Silva had other ideas and he came within a whisker of inspiring an incredible fight-back.

Firstly he pulled a goal back on 57 minutes and then, five minutes later, his low cross was deflected in to his own net by Glen Johnson and the icing on the cake so nearly came on 75 minutes as Sergio Aguero broke free on the left before sending a low cross into the middle where Silva slid in to agonisingly send the ball just wide. The pass had been slightly too heavy or else City would have taken the lead. As it was, Philippe Coutinho scored what would be the decisive goal just three minutes later to send Anfield wild. City's destiny was no longer in their own hands with Liverpool seven points clear at the top.

Silva was City's chief tormentor against fellow title hopefuls Liverpool, but a defeat in spite of his efforts, followed by a crushing injury blow in the win over West Brom (right), meant the task of chasing down the Merseysiders at the top of the table would become much tougher

The Blues still had two games in hand, but a demoralising 2-2 draw with bogey team Sunderland just a few days later meant City had to hope both Chelsea and Liverpool stumbled in their final few games. Silva had been playing with an injured ankle and missed the game with Sunderland, and the decision to play him in the next game – a 3-1 win over West Brom – seemed to have badly backfired as he was carried off on a stretcher in the second half. It was a sobering sight for the City fans who gave him a standing ovation as he left the pitch and the task ahead suddenly looked that much harder.

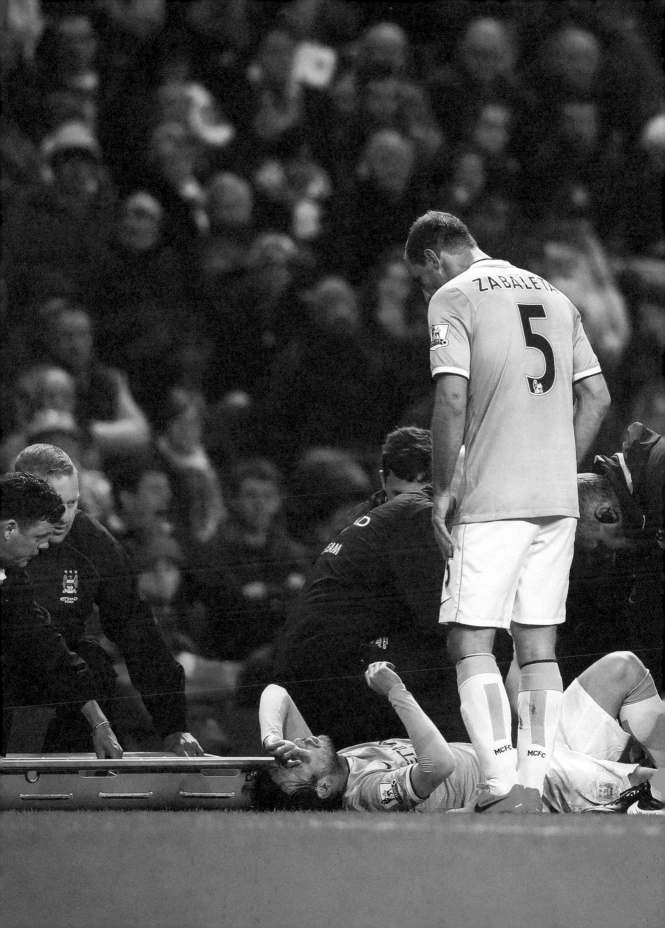

After a brief injury lay-off, Silva was back, and so was City's title belief, especially after his excellent build-up play resulted in two goals for Dzeko (right) in a 4-0 penultimate Premier League win over Aston Villa

# "If Liverpool win 14 games in a row they deserve to be champions but our duty is to win all our games"

After the game, Manuel Pellegrini said: "David Silva was playing the games before with the problem in his ankle and that's why he couldn't play against Sunderland, but we'll see on Tuesday with the doctor what injury he has. If Liverpool win 14 games in a row they deserve to be champions but our duty is to obligate them to win all their games. We'll see what they do, but our duty is to win all our games. In the second half we tried to keep the result but the team played the way we have the whole year."

The diagnosis was rest and recovery, but with the title suddenly back on after Chelsea's 2-0 win at Anfield, City had been unexpectedly thrown a lifeline – and needed the inspirational Silva more than ever. He sat out the 2-0 win at Crystal Palace that put Pellegrini's side within three points of Liverpool, but he was back on the bench after painkilling injections for the crucial trip to Goodison Park where City edged a tense game to win 3-2 and move to the top of the table. Incredibly, Liverpool would throw a 3-0 lead away against Crystal Palace two days later – the Eagles scoring all their goals in the last 10 minutes – leaving City needing four points from the last two games (bar a wild swing in goal difference Liverpool's way).

Silva was up for the task and, as he always did, put the team over his own welfare with his ankle problem still giving him severe discomfort, started the penultimate game of the season against Aston Villa. It proved a much more difficult game than expected, with Villa defending in numbers and holding out until midway

A final push from Silva in the 2-0 win over West Ham helps City over the finish line as Premier League champions

through the second half when, inevitably, Silva was at the heart of the move that saw City take the lead.

His sublime pass opened up the Villa defence for Zabaleta to get in behind and cross for Dzeko to finally break the deadlock. Eight minutes later, Silva again put Zabaleta in behind and his low cross found Samir Nasri whose shot was saved but Dzeko was on hand to score his second of the night.

David's work was complete for the evening as he left the pitch to a now customary standing ovation on 76 minutes. Two more late goals from Stevan Jovetic and Yaya Toure completed a 4-0 win and left City needing one point from the final game against West Ham United at the Etihad. Again, Silva played his part despite the discomfort, and goals from Samir Nasri and Vincent Kompany meant he could walk off to a thunderous reception yet again with 76 minutes played.

"It's been a long and tough year but we are champions again, so I am very happy. There have been so many teams fighting to the end, but we won it, which makes it even more satisfying"

City were champions for the second time in three years and, while it had been a superb team effort, Silva had been the driving force of what had been an incredible burst to the finish line. His 40 appearances had yielded eight goals and 16 assists in all competitions and yet he wasn't considered worthy of a PFA Player of the Year nomination for 2014, though three Liverpool players and Yaya Toure (deservedly) did. It would be a familiar pattern for *El Mago*.

After the game, he said, "I am so happy for the fans who have supported us wholeheartedly all season. And I am happy for the whole squad. It's been a long and tough year but we are champions again, so I am very happy. There have been so many teams fighting to the end, but we won it, which makes it even more satisfying. In the back of our minds, we remembered 2012 and winning it at the last minute, so that kept us going."

It had been another unforgettable campaign for a player with a heart as big as the island he was born on and his unusual mix of artistry and courage was making him a Manchester City legend, just four years into his stay…

The victory parade through the streets of Manchester marks the end of another successful campaign for Silva and City

**Pride in Battle**

SILVA
MEMORIES
2013/14

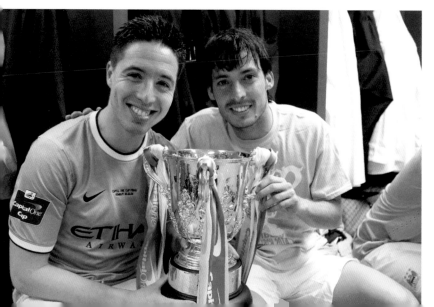

161

*Temporadas de cambios*

# Seasons of change

# "HE RUNS THE GAME. HIS SECOND GOAL WAS A LOVELY FINISH. HE IS TRULY EXCEPTIONAL. A JOY TO WATCH"

Spain's world dominance had ended during the summer of 2014, with *La Roja* dumped out of the World Cup in the group stages of the tournament held in Brazil. David Silva featured in all three games, but a 5-1 loss to Holland and a 2-0 defeat to Chile meant the 3-0 victory over Australia in the final group fixture was too little, too late. If nothing else, it gave the City playmaker a longer than expected summer break after pretty much four years of constant football.

Manuel Pellegrini didn't add any major new faces to his squad and Alvaro Negredo would be shipped back to Valencia in September having failed to rediscover his blistering form from the first half of the previous season, largely due to a shoulder injury sustained at the end of January.

As for David Silva, City again ensured their prized asset was tied to another improved, long-term contract in August 2014. Silva's new deal was a five-year contract that would keep him in Manchester until the end of the 2019 campaign at least. It was a huge statement from the Club and the player that this was a long-term and mutual desire. It also meant that, when the deal expired, he would be 33 and so was committing his best years to City and, perhaps the remainder of his career.

On announcing the deal, he said: "From the moment I joined the

# "It was a straightforward decision to extend my stay here and spend my peak years at Manchester City, a club with unbelievable fans who have always supported me"

Club four years ago, it has felt like a second home to me. On and off the pitch, I feel incredibly content and fulfilled professionally and personally, so why wouldn't I want to stay and keep winning trophies with this fantastic team? Over the last four years, we have achieved so much together, establishing City as a dominating force in England and now, when I look around this dressing room, I can see no reason why we won't become one of the top teams in the world. It was a straightforward decision to extend my stay here and spend my peak years at Manchester City, a club with unbelievable fans who have always supported me."

Just as with City's previous two title-winning campaigns, there seemed to be something of a hangover going into the 2014/15 campaign – David's fifth with the Club. Silva was on target in the opening day 2-0 win at Newcastle and the Blues were again impressive when swatting away Liverpool at the Etihad eight days later. But a 1-0 home loss to Stoke and successive draws against Arsenal and Chelsea took the shine off the start, though City would stay in touch with leaders Chelsea, winning four of the next five games, but one thing that was emerging with great clarity was that opposing teams were targeting Silva. It wasn't completely a case of 'stop Silva, stop City', but if he wasn't pulling the strings for club or country, victory against Pellegrini's side was more achievable.

Silva wheels away in celebration after stroking home the opening goal of City's 2014/15 Premier League campaign at Newcastle, but the City star would suffer contrasting fortunes the next time he took on the Tynesiders...

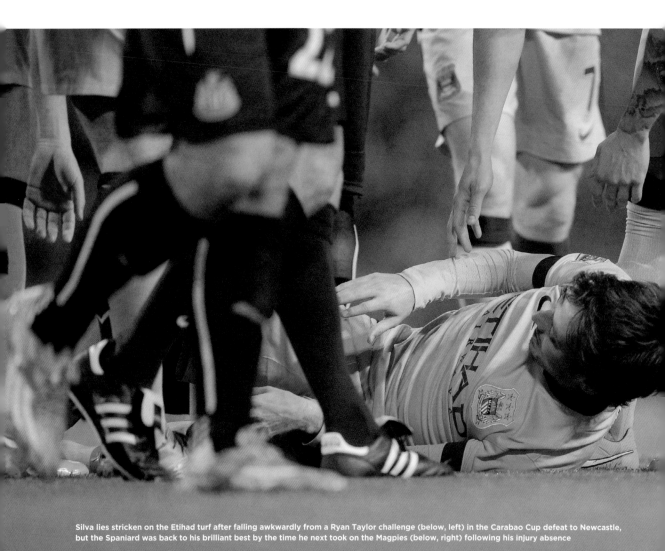

Silva lies stricken on the Etihad turf after falling awkwardly from a Ryan Taylor challenge (below, left) in the Carabao Cup defeat to Newcastle, but the Spaniard was back to his brilliant best by the time he next took on the Magpies (below, right) following his injury absence

He needed protecting and, when necessary, resting – so some questioned the wisdom of manager Manuel Pellegrini when he named Silva in his starting XI for the Capital One Cup tie with a much-changed Newcastle United. If ever there was an occasion to give your most prized asset the night off, that game was surely it. The Chilean had made seven changes, but decided to start Silva and in doing so, took a gamble – and lost. Just a few minutes in, Silva was challenged by Ryan Taylor on the edge of the box and went down awkwardly.

Although he got up and played on for a few moments, with just nine on the clock, he sat down on the turf, unable to continue. The injury would sideline him for six weeks.

By February, Silva was back in full flow and trying to drive City towards another title, but Chelsea had hit the front early and were showing little sign of encountering a blip. A 5-0 win over Newcastle at the Etihad left City five points behind the leaders with a dozen games to go – Silva had a hand in four of the goals, assisting one directly for Edin Dzeko and scoring two in three minutes himself just after the break.

Dzeko said after the game: "The pass from David was first class, and for me he is the best player in the Premier League. To have him here with us is amazing. With David, you can always score goals.

"We played an amazing game knowing that we are playing a big game in three days against Barcelona in the Champions League. Our defence enjoyed this game and so did I. We knew that Chelsea had only drawn [with Burnley and we had to do our job today. We did it well. People say five points is a lot [big gap to Chelsea] and maybe it is, but if we keep playing like we did today then I think we can definitely catch them. First of all, we have to concentrate and try and win our games."

Watching Sky Sports pundit Jamie Redknapp was equally impressed by Silva's display against the Magpies. He said: "He is absolutely exceptional. The little man (Silva) was involved in everything, but he was given the freedom of the park. He is the maestro; he knows where the passes are going to go. He runs the game. His second goal was a lovely finish. He is truly exceptional. A joy to watch."

And the superlatives didn't end there.

It had generally been accepted that Colin Bell was City's greatest player of all time, but the former attacking midfielder, who clocked up almost 500 appearances for City during his playing days insisted that the crown of greatest player should be passed on to David Silva.

Said Bell: "David Silva would walk into any City team of any era. He is in my personal greatest all-time XI and is just fantastic to watch. When he's on the ball, he makes the whole team tick and we don't look the same side without him. He has an incredible awareness and is the perfect player for the modern game.

"People ask me how I rate him compared to the players who played during my era and he's up there with the very best. We were different players – don't get me wrong – and I suppose I brought something different to the City team than David does. My game was more about box-to-box, high energy with a lot of running, but that's not how the game is now.

"Silva glides around the pitch and is an integral part of our recent successes and he is a genuine pleasure to watch. I used to tackle more and head it, but he doesn't need to do that side of the game because there are other players in the team who do that. All you need to do is give him the ball and he takes care of the rest. I suppose I was more of an all-rounder in that respect, but as I say, the game has changed a lot in the past 30 years or so."

For Silva, it was one of the ultimate accolades. Well aware of Bell's playing career and standing among City fans, he admitted that his words had meant a lot to him.

"I'm just focused on playing, but the opinion that really matters to me is the one of the City fans who watch our games every week," said David. "That said, obviously, when people talk well about you positively, it's always helpful because it means you are doing well and it's beautiful when people appreciate your work. Of course, when you are not doing so well you have to accept the criticism as well! For me, it was really nice to hear what Colin Bell said recently. I appreciate his opinion highly because he is a very important former player from the Club's past. He's a legend and receiving those words from such an important player for the City and England makes me very happy, honoured, and I appreciate it a lot."

Sadly for City, despite Silva's form, the season unravelled quickly after the win over Newcastle. Defeat to Barcelona in the Champions League Round of 16 meant that, after early exits in both domestic cup competitions, the Premier League became the sole focus for Pellegrini's men, but four defeats in six matches left City 12 behind adrift of Chelsea with only six matches remaining. The title challenge was over. Only by winning those remaining half-dozen games did City manage to secure runners-up spot and salvage something out of what had ultimately ended up a disappointing campaign.

David had still managed 12 goals and 10 assists, but there were no more winner's medals to add to his collection.

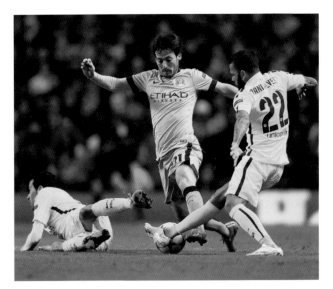

The Champions League defeat to Barcelona in March meant focus for Silva and City was on chasing down Chelsea in the Premier League

Silva twists and turns his way
through the West Brom defence
as he makes an impressive start
to the 2015/16 season

# "It is very important to start the season with a win. David really played well. It was an unbelievable performance. He did not make any mistakes"

The 2015/16 season would be one of contrasts, injuries and ultimately, something of a damp squib. None of that had seemed a possibility when City roared out of the blocks to win an opening day win at West Brom and for the third year in succession, David scored the Blues' opening goal of the campaign. Pellegrini hailed Silva's display, saying: "It is very important to start the season with a win and to win in the way we did – scoring goals and playing as a very consistent team without giving West Brom any real chances to score – is pleasing. I enjoy seeing technical players play well. David really played well – especially in the first-half. It was an unbelievable performance. He did not make any mistakes."

City would go on to win their opening five Premier League games and moved five points clear at the top of the table. It could hardly have gone any better and David was convinced it signalled another strong title challenge for the Blues.

"I'm just very happy because the team has started very well," said Silva. "We've won our first five games but I'm also happy because the team is showing a very good style of play. The first season we won the title in 2011/12, we also started really well and kept going right up until December and then finished very strongly. I hope this will be the same again this year. We must give everything we have but take it game by game. We will need some luck on our side at times, too, but we are pleased with the way things are going."

Silva played in City's 6-1 win over Newcastle at the start of October, but it would be his last club game for eight weeks. Scythed down by Luxembourg's Lars Gerson with just 10 minutes gone while on duty for Spain, David left the field with a sprained ankle and City faced up to eight weeks without his services. With Sergio Aguero also ruled out for six weeks and Vincent Kompany's continuing muscle injuries recurring, it left City arguably without the services of their three best players during the autumn.

A chastening 4-1 home defeat to a rampant Liverpool suggested Pellegrini's City weren't going to challenge for the Premier League title and by the time the Blues lost 2-1 at Arsenal, City had won just five of their previous 12 league games and fallen six points behind surprise leaders Leicester City.

At the time, David said: "When the team is in a bad run, the next game is difficult because you need to react, get some confidence and get back to winning ways," he said.

A lunging tackle from Lars Gerson during Spain's October international with Luxembourg resulted in another enforced injury absence for Silva

Four wins and three draws put City back on course in the league and with qualification for the Champions League Round of 16 and a Carabao Cup final place against Liverpool already in the bag, there was plenty to be optimistic about – even more so, when at the start of February, the Club announced that, to quell continued speculation and uncertainty, Pep Guardiola would become the new manager at the end of the 2015/16 season.

Coincidental or not, City would

**Silva helps guide City
into the last four of the
2015/16 Champions League
following the quarter-final
triumph over PSG**

# "We won the league title for the first time in 44 years and then wanted to go further in the Champions League, and that's a reality now"

lose four of the next seven Premier League games and fall 15 points behind leaders Leicester City, but beaten Liverpool to win the Capital One Cup on penalties and reached the quarter-finals of the Champions League for the first time where Paris Saint-Germain awaited. The Blues secured a 2-2 draw in Paris and Kevin De Bruyne's lone strike in the return set up a semi-final with Real Madrid – the team that had allowed David to slip through their grasp as a teenager.

After the win over PSG, Silva was in no doubt that City had earned their crack at the Spanish giants: "We protected the result we achieved in Paris and tonight, they didn't create many chances. We even missed a penalty kick and produced some good counter-attacks until Kevin scored at the perfect time.

"We never stopped believing, even when Sergio missed. We just keep going. The match is very long and despite the penalty, the team was very focused from start to finish. The manager is very happy but now we have to think about Saturday's game against Chelsea. We have two league games in a very short space of time and we have to perform well.

"It's not easy to get to the semi-final but we are doing the right things. We won the title for the first time in 44 years and then wanted to go further in the Champions League, and that's a reality now. Any team we may play in the semi-finals will be tough so we'll be happy being drawn with anyone.

David's season comes to an end after sustaining an ankle injury in the Champions League semi-final with Real Madrid

"It's difficult to win the Premier League, but we have to try to finish as high in the table as we can and secure Champions League football for the next season. We've had two tough games against a great side. We played well in Paris and got a good result which has helped us to be more relaxed here tonight."

For many, City's hopes of winning the Champions League ended 40 minutes into the first leg against Real Madrid when David Silva's season also ended. He limped off with an ankle injury and would not play again that season. City drew the game 0-0 and lost the return 1-0 in Madrid meaning David had been denied the stage he had deserved, back on Spanish soil, with the opportunity to progress to the Champions League final. In the second leg, City were tentative, lacked fluency and, at times, devoid of creativity. We can only imagine what might have been had Silva been fit.

As it was, the next time he pulled on a City shirt, it would be with Pep Guardiola as his manager. Silva and Pep – it felt like an irresistible combination.

# DAVID SILVA EL MAGO

# SILVA
## MEMORIES
### 2014/15

SILVA MEMORIES

2015/16

*Dirigiendo una sinfonía*

# Conducting
# a symphony

# "I FEEL GOOD, HAPPY, THAT I'VE PLAYED SO MANY GAMES FOR CITY MEANS I'M GETTING A BIT OLDER NOW, BUT I'M HAPPY HERE"

Pep Guardiola's arrival at City initially had people wondering whether he would bring in his own players and what the future was for players such as David Silva. Those worries proved unfounded. Pep had been an admirer of Silva for many years and in the system the Catalan boss favoured – 4-3-3 or variations of that – David was to play a key role, and though there would be no silverware in Pep's first season, the former Barcelona manager was figuring out what was needed to shape the sort of team capable of playing his brand of football.

As for *El Mago*, playing under Pep Guardiola was a joy and though the 2016/17 campaign was his seventh in sky blue, his consistency and artistry levels never wavered – if anything, they went up a notch. And if Vincent Kompany or Pablo Zabaleta didn't play, it was David who Pep chose to captain his team. It proved to be a season of transition, but an enjoyable and productive one, nonetheless.

"With a coach like Pep, you learn a lot"

"I feel good, happy," said Silva. "That I've played so many games for City means I'm getting a bit older now, but I'm happy here, I feel comfortable and I hope to play many more games and that things go well for me and the Club. I feel proud of having worn the armband, but I have always said that after so many years in a club or with your national team, even if you don't wear it, you feel important and you try to help the younger players.

"And that's how I feel now, and I want to help the younger players the same way I was helped when I arrived here or when I started at Valencia or wherever I've been. People have helped me and I'm trying to do so now. You always want to help the team in whatever way you can.

"With a coach like Pep, you learn a lot, to be honest. After all these years in football and with my experience... after four or five months with him I have learnt a lot, even when you are at an age where you think you can't learn much more, then you do and you start looking at things from a different point of view. He's an exceptional manager and I'm thoroughly enjoying playing football under him.

"It is true that I am playing some steps further back sometimes because I have to help in the build-up, but Guardiola also gives me freedom to attack and be close to our opponents' goal and create chances, which is something that I

The arrival of Pep Guardiola as City boss marked another era of excellence from Silva

really enjoy. He gives me a lot of freedom and I am very happy playing in this role. The manager wants us to control the game, create chances in front of goal, control the rival team with the counter-attacks and be ready to neutralise that. I think we're doing great and I hope we can continue like that."

City started incredibly well under Guardiola – perhaps too well, with expectations going through the roof, despite the Catalan's warning not to expect his side to sweep all before them. At least not yet. By early December, City had lost to – and beaten – Barcelona on the way to the Champions League Round of 16, but a 3-1 home defeat to Chelsea in a bad-tempered game at the Etihad proved pivotal, with the West London side going top and City dropping to fourth.

The season proved an entertaining one, but the Blues were never in serious contention for the title during the second half of the campaign. The Champions League adventure ended at the Round

of 16 stage with a thrilling 6-6 aggregate score against Monaco seeing the Ligue 1 side progress on away goals and Arsenal ended City's FA Cup hopes with a 2-1 win in the semi-final at Wembley. Third spot was secured on the final day of the campaign with a 5-0 win away to Watford and David ended the season having played 52 games for club and country, scoring 12 goals and assisting 10 more.

He was voted the Etihad Manchester City Player of the Year for 2016/17 – incredibly, it was the first time he had won the coveted prize, voted for by City supporters.

City's Ambassador Mike Summerbee said at the time: "It's a bold statement to make when you consider players from different eras

FA Cup semi-final defeat to Arsenal (above) was the closest David came to more silverware during a season of transition under Guardiola, while Chelsea's fiery 3-1 win at the Etihad in December (right) helped the Londoners secure honours in the Premier League

"I think you learn to value the important things in life. Football was the thing that helped me the most. For that time I was out on the field, those 90 minutes, that was the only time I could forget stuff" and so on but I believe David Silva to be the greatest player to ever wear a City shirt. He has been getting the recognition he deserves off pundits just lately and yet he never wins the Man-of-the-Match award, which is odd, because I think he's the best player on the pitch every time I see him play. Moreover, he's a genuinely nice, generous and humble man and he thoroughly deserves this award."

The 2017/18 campaign would prove to be one of incredible highs and lows for David.

On the pitch, here was a player at the very peak of his powers, effortlessly knitting play between defence and attack and so often the pass before the assist would come from the telepathic vision of David Silva. The football Guardiola's City were playing was sensational and by mid-December, David had played 23 games for club and country, winning 22 of those games and drawing the other. There had been 67 goals scored in that spell – an average slightly better than three per game and, in football terms, Gran Canaria's most famous export was having the time of his life.

But football was about to become irrelevant, as David learned his partner Yessica had given birth prematurely and a baby son, Mateo, who was now fighting for his life.

Pep Guardiola told David to forget about football and come back only when it was right for him. There was no pressure on him to play and no matter how long it took, the Club were 100 per cent behind him and would support him in any way possible. Perhaps to relieve the anxiety and stress of the situation, David split his time between Manchester and the Casa de Salud hospital in Valencia, spending as much time as he could with Mateo and his partner at the hospital and flying back to play here and there, continually talking with doctors and taking their advice on Mateo's condition.

"I think you learn to value the important things in life," David reflected. "I don't waste my time doing my head in about stupid things that don't really matter and don't waste time worrying over nothing. So, yeah, it puts things in perspective. It's funny, it's a question I ask myself – how did I cope with that? Football was actually the thing that helped me the most. For that time I was out on the field, those 90 minutes, that was the only way, the only time I could forget stuff. For that short time, you'd enjoy the game for what it was but then, as soon as it is over, you're back to thinking about everything again."

The first game he missed was at home to Tottenham in December, and Pep sent out City with the clear instructions that they were to win it for their team-mate. David, watching the 4-1 win on his iPad from hospital, says he will never forget the outpouring of support and well wishes from the dressing room, and as Kevin De Bruyne rifled home City's second of the game on 70 minutes, he ran to the pitch-side camera and held two fingers up on one hand and one on the other to form '21'.

"It's something I'll be grateful for forever," said David. "I don't think anyone

Silva had the premature birth of his son Mateo to deal with during the 2017/18 season, but messages of support – including the one sent by Kevin De Bruyne in the win over Spurs, helped David come through a tough time far stronger

can ever be prepared for something like that. Until you physically go through that situation, you can't appreciate what it would be like. Everyone has an image of a premature child, but until you live it and experience it, you just don't know how bad it is."

Thankfully, as the weeks and months passed, Mateo became stronger and was eventually allowed to leave the hospital. The football, meanwhile, could hardly have been going any better with City running away with the Premier League title. David also played and scored in the 3-0 Carabao Cup triumph at Wembley and by the end of March, City knew victory over Manchester United in

## DAVID SILVA EL MAGO

Premier League title celebrations brought to a close a testing City campaign for Silva who would make the last of his 125 Spain appearances that summer at the 2018 World Cup

"The national team gave me everything and helped me grow as a player and a person. I leave proud and happy, bringing an end to a time full of emotions and memories"

the first week of April would secure a third Premier league title in six years. The Blues would lose the game 3-2, but it merely delayed the inevitable and the title was confirmed a couple of weeks later with a 5-0 win over Swansea – with David grabbing the opening goal of the rout.

City refused to take their foot off the gas in the games that remained and broke numerous Club and Premier League records on the way to reaching 100 points on the final day of the season against Southampton. With 10 goals and 14 assists from his season with City and Mateo getting stronger all the time, Silva was ready for the 2018 World Cup in Ukraine. He had again made the shortlist for the PFA Player of the Year – along with team-mates Kevin De Bruyne and Leroy Sane – and was also selected in the PFA Team of the Year; incredible feats considering the personal issues he'd had to deal with.

# SILVA
## MEMORIES
### 2016/17

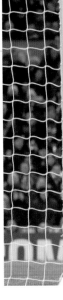

# SILVA
## MEMORIES
### 2017/18

# The perfect 10

*Los diez perfectos*

David shows off his son Mateo at the Etihad as the Blues get their 2018/19 home campaign under way

# "I CAN NEVER SEE MYSELF PLAYING AGAINST CITY FOR ANOTHER TEAM. SO 10 YEARS – THAT'S IT."

**D**avid left for the Spain World Cup training camp already knowing it would be his swansong for La Roja. Spain were far from the side that dominated world football for four years between 2008 and 2012, but they were still expected to reach the latter stages of the tournament in Russia. He would feature in all Spain's games up until he left the pitch after 67 minutes of the Round of 16 tie with hosts Russia, replaced by close friend Andres Iniesta. Russia won the game 4-3 on penalties.

Though he was only 32, he decided it was time for others to have their chance in the national team while he focused on City and his young family. The international breaks would become a time to recharge his batteries and spend more time with his loved ones and after 12 years representing his country, 125 caps and 35 goals, he was the sixth most capped Spanish international of all time and the fourth highest goal-scorer, too.

It had been an incredible international career and he announced it was over on social media, saying: "I lived and dreamed with a team that will forever be remembered. It has not been easy, after all I've experienced, to write these lines. I've spent days and weeks considering this. The national team gave me everything and helped me grow as a player and a person. I leave proud and happy, bringing

"When he was in hospital, I dreamed of that moment when I could carry him out with me at the Etihad"

an end to a time full of emotions and memories, like the figure of Luis Aragonés, a maestro who will never be forgotten."

After returning to Gran Canaria for a break with his family and friends, David returned to Manchester to prepare for the 2018/19 season, where Pep Guardiola's side would attempt to defend the Premier League title. Though he didn't play as City secured the FA Community Shield against Chelsea or in the 2-0 opening day Premier League win at Arsenal, David led the team out for the opening home game of the campaign against Huddersfield Town carrying baby Mateo in his arms. It felt like the end of an arduous journey for all concerned, but one with a very happy ending. "When he was in hospital, I dreamed of that moment when I could carry him out with me at the Etihad," he revealed.

It was a proud and emotional moment and the day would only get better, as David curled a beautiful free-kick home on 48 minutes and celebrated by waving to his son in the Colin Bell Stand in a game City went on to win 6-1.

David curls home a free-kick
against Huddersfield Town
on an emotional day

Celebrating a goal against Manchester United and *(opposite right)* against West Ham. Silva scored in four successive games in November 2018

By late November, after scoring for a fourth successive game in a row, David had bagged eight goals in his first 17 games and was easily on his way to his best ever tally. Few disagreed that he was playing some of the best football of his career and his decision to retire from international duty was proving inspired. And City needed David Silva at his best as the defending Premier League champions slugged out an absorbing title race with Liverpool.

City were playing scintillating, free-flowing football and Silva was the beating heart of a relentless machine, but Liverpool were equal to almost everything the Blues did and would even edge ahead at the top from December onwards. Ironically, after his free-scoring start to the season, he would score just two more in his next 33 games, but his contribution was never less than superb during that time.

He played 79 minutes of City's Carabao Cup final win over Chelsea and though the Champions League dream ended with a dramatic quarter-final loss to Tottenham, City were clawing their way back in the title race and had also booked a place in the FA

Cup final. The title race would continue until the last kick of the season, with City just edging the race with Liverpool by one point.

But the season wasn't over. David opened the scoring in the 26th-minute of the FA Cup final against Watford to become only the second City player to score in an FA Cup final and a League Cup final – and he received a standing ovation when he left the pitch on 79 minutes with the Blues already 4-0 up. Within the space of a few weeks, he'd added two more winner's medals to his sizeable collection as City completed an unprecedented domestic clean sweep of all four trophies.

He had made 50 appearances for the Club – his second-best tally – as well as equalling his best goals haul of 10. It had been a remarkable season for the now 33-year-old and for the first time in his professional career, he could look forward to a complete rest over the summer with no international commitments. He was entering the final year of his current deal, and though City were keen to extend his stay beyond 2020, he had already made another difficult decision.

In June 2019, he revealed that the last year of his current deal with City would also be his final year with the Club. "This is the last one," he revealed in an interview in Gran Canaria. "Ten years for me is enough. It's the perfect time for me. Initially, City were talking about two [more] years. It completes the cycle. It's a nice round figure. I can never see myself playing against City for another team. So 10 years – that's it."

The words City fans had dreaded hearing were finally a reality. He had won four Premier League titles, two FA Cups, five League Cups and three FA Community Shields while with City and it was perhaps only a Champions League winner's medal that was the notable absentee from his personal collection. David returned to City for pre-season training in July and following Vincent

Silva became only the second City player to score in an FA Cup final and a League Cup final

Celebrating with the Premier League title after a dramatic last day victory at Brighton

Kompany's departure, his team-mates voted him to be the new captain. The Club had a new leader and, now 33, Silva couldn't have been any prouder to have taken on the skipper's armband for City.

He had the total respect of everyone at the Club – manager, team-mates, staff and supporters – and he was determined to enjoy what would be his final campaign in sky blue. He initially led the team out at Wembley in the Community Shield clash with Liverpool and assisted Raheem Sterling's goal as City eventually won the game on penalties.

Pep Guardiola later confirmed what everybody had second-guessed when he admitted, "David Silva will be our captain.

"Normally, the captain is the life of the locker room. The players know each other; they have fun a lot when they are together. There will be no problem. He will be a good captain."

Indeed he is. The 2019/20 season remains unfinished as the Club decided to release this tribute while David was still a Manchester City player.

David led the team out for the Community Shield against Liverpool which City won on penalties

He turned 34 in January 2020, though you'd never guess it. One thing that is for certain is that he will have moved into the Club's all-time Top 10 for appearances, which in this day and age is incredible. Prior to our Premier League game against Arsenal in March 2020, 'El Mago' was on 422 appearances in all competitions.

"Ten years for me is enough. It's the perfect time for me"

"It's hard to imagine a
Manchester City side without
David Silva in it"

No.10 in the list is Willie Donachie with 425, so it's safe to say David will pass that number.

He has also scored 73 goals and assisted an incredible 137 goals for his team-mates. He is our most decorated player with 13 trophies and possibly one or two more to come. It's hard to imagine a Manchester City side without David Silva in it and when he claimed that joining the Club was the best decision of his career, we can only say that one of Manchester City's best decisions was signing David Silva.

A genuine Club legend. It has been a privilege, *El Mago*…

# SILVA
## MEMORIES
### 2018/19

# SILVA
MEMORIES

2019/20

### ROBERTO CARLOS

Left-back

"Like Cafu, Roberto is very attacking and has won many titles for club and country. For me, he is one of the best ever."

### CARLOS PUYOL

Centre-back

"Another player I have enjoyed great success alongside. He is a great defender and very brave."

### LUIS FIGO

Left-wing

"Figo would be my left-sided attacking midfielder/ winger – he could play on either side and he was great at one-on-ones."

### IKER CASILLAS

Goalkeeper

"I've won many titles with him and, for me, he is the best."

### SERGIO RAMOS

Centre-back

"For the same reasons as Casillas, really. I've played many times with him in the national team, we've won many titles together and I think he is one of the best defenders in the world."

### Forward

## RONALDO

"I would go for the Brazilian Ronaldo. He has won everything including the World Cup and was the best in his position. He is the best striker I have ever seen."

### Forward

## LIONEL MESSI

"For me, he is the greatest player in the world. I haven't had the chance to see some of the other world greats, really but I have seen a lot of Messi."

### Right-back

## CAFU

"Another player who has won many titles and the World Cup. I like him because he is very attack-minded."

### Midfielder

## PATRICK VIEIRA

"He has won so much and was a fantastic defensive midfielder. I was lucky enough to play with him towards the end of his career at City."

### Midfielder

## CLAUDE MAKELELE

"He would be able to hold the midfield and was a great, combative midfielder."

### Right-wing

## MICHAEL LAUDRUP

"Laudrup would have to go on the right of midfield – he was my idol so I would have to pick him, no matter what!"

# David's Dream XI 4-4-2

## THIS IS THE LINE-UP HE SUGGESTED WHEN HE WAS PREVIOUSLY ASKED TO NAME HIS DREAM TEAM ...

# Why 21LVA?

David Silva has always worn the No.21 jersey during his time at City. He also wore it at Eibar, Valencia and for Spain – but what is the reason always coveted that particular squad number for club and country?

"I moved to Eibar a very short time before the beginning of the 2004/05 season and it was the only one available," Silva revealed. "It was given to me. Then I moved to Celta on loan and 21 was already taken, so I took the number 16. Afterwards, I went back to Valencia and 19 and 21 were the only numbers left.

"I was wearing the 21 before and it was also the one of Pablo Aimar at Valencia, a player which, in terms of playing style, was the most similar to me, so I wanted it for myself. And here's an anecdote I never told to Jaime Gavilan. That year when both of us arrived there, 19 and 21 were the only squad numbers available, and I got on really well with Curro Torres.

Childhood hero Valeron wore the No.21 shirt

"Me and Gavilan, both newcomers, held a raffle and in a moment when he was distracted, Curro told me which one to pick. It was hidden in his hands and I picked the one with the 21.

"We cheated a little bit there… and Gavi was never aware of that. And I've been wearing the 21 shirt until now… and I never told him! I hope he will understand…"

Silva's first love of the No.21 shirt came from watching his idols

Juan Carlos Valeron and Michael Laudrup. Like Silva, of course, Valeron was born in Arguineguin, Gran Canaria, and possessed outstanding technical ability. Valeron went on to have a top-level career in La Liga with Mallorca, Atletico Madrid and Deportivo la Coruna, as well as winning 46 caps for Spain.

Meanwhile, Denmark legend Laudrup, a European Cup winner with Barcelona who also won five La Liga titles during a distinguished playing career, was considered one of the finest dribblers the game has ever seen – something that, as explained earlier, left an indelible impression on a young David Silva.

"Juan Carlos Valeron and his brother Miguel Angel, both played with my dad in Arguineguin," Silva recalled. "Juan Carlos was always a role model to me. I knew him and he was an incredible person. And then it was Laudrup. I've always said that he was my childhood idol. Both were a major influence reference for me."

# 21 PIECES OF SILVA: WHAT THEY SAY...

## #01/21:
## PEP GUARDIOLA

"He has been one of the greats, not only in Spanish football, but in European football as well. He has played for 10 years in Manchester and it is not easy to perform in that league for someone with his qualities. He has done incredibly well. He helped me personally, he has helped us a lot in these three years we have been together. We have another year more and I hope we can enjoy another good year together."

**#02/21:**
**THIERRY HENRY**

"He's the best creative midfielder we've seen in this league. I didn't see everyone play, but David Silva wants the ball and plays the same way against every team. He puts his foot in and doesn't shy away from the ball. He's brave off the ball and on the ball. What a player."

**#03/21:**
# GARY NEVILLE

"David Silva is a player who is quite unique because he neutralises every single football fan and professional football player in the country. Everybody, universally, just loves him."

## #04/21:
## VINCENT KOMPANY

"One thing David will have done is change the way Man City fans look at football. I think you had a lot of players come here — like I did, like Pablo Zabaleta did — but David Silva made sure there's now another element that City fans expect to their football."

**#05/21:**
**MARIO BALOTELLI**

"He's the slow Messi! That
says everything"

**#06/21:**
**VICENTE DEL BOSQUE**

"David Silva is our Lionel
Messi!"

**#07/21:**
**XAVI**

"David Silva is one of the most talented players Spain has ever produced, without a shadow of a doubt."

## #08/21:
## YAYA TOURE

"I was on the phone with chief executive Garry Cook. He promised me he was going to bring players to help me do great things at City. I said, 'Sign David Silva from Valencia first, and I will come.' And Silva was saying, 'Sign Yaya first and I will come!' I said to Silva, 'Sign! I am not going to run off!'

### #09/21:
# JAMIE CARRAGHER

"Silva is Manchester City's greatest ever player. The one disappointment is his age — how long is he going to play? He's alongside Thierry Henry, Dennis Bergkamp and Eric Cantona — he's one of the greatest we've ever had in the Premier League."

### #10/21:
# CARLOS TEVEZ

"David Silva is the best signing we have made. He is the type of player who can win you the game. He can provide you with the sort of pass that puts you through one on one with the goalkeeper. He's one of the best players in the squad. He has freshened up the team and brought a new dimension to it."

## #11/21:
# FRANK LAMPARD

"I'd put him right in the top bracket of the best players I've played with in my career. I've been fortunate enough to play alongside players like Gianfranco Zola, Arjen Robben and Eden Hazard among others, and he's completely up there with the best. From the moment I arrived and started training with him in pre-season, I could better appreciate his weight of pass, movement, and his touch and he could play in any team in the world.

"It's been a pleasure to play and train alongside him or even just to watch him. The way he holds himself, too, impresses me because he's one of the humblest top players I've ever come across — that's something I love because it's refreshing to see. To be at the top of your game, have all the medals he has and do what he does week in, week out, and yet it's still like he's just coming in, doing his day job and going home."

**#12/21:**
# ANDRES INIESTA

"He pulls the strings on the pitch. A brilliant footballer with great movement, he can score, assist; he's a player who decides a game. He's got so much to his game that I would consider him one of the best ever."

## #13/21:
## PATRICK VIEIRA

"Since he joined the Club, I don't think we have really said enough how good he is. He is one of the best players in the world, no doubt about it. For me, he is up there. When you talk about Messi and Ronaldo, yes they are fantastic, but David can be put in the same category of players who could play in any team around the world. His football brain, his ability to control the ball and play football, is unbelievable. I am a huge fan.

"When the team is struggling, that is when the leaders come out, and David showed he is a leader. He may be very quiet but when he is on the field, he takes the responsibility, and that is the kind of leader you need in your team."

## #14/21:
## SERGIO AGUERO

"David is one of the true pillars of this team. Since I arrived, we were able to click inside and outside the field.

"He's one of the team-mates who I see eye-to-eye with the most to this day. Of course, I'd always prefer to play with David on my team, but all things come to an end, don't they? We'll all enjoy every last minute he's able to play on our side, myself included, and then we'll miss him dearly when he's gone. Players like David, who consistently give it all throughout the years, will always be a part of this Club."

**#15/21:**
**KEVIN DE BRUYNE**

"On the ball, David Silva is amazing. He can do everything and dictate the tempo of a game from start to finish, so he's a great player to have when you want control of the game — I'd say that's one of his best traits. He has great vision, can find anyone with a pass and it is great to have him as a team-mate."

# #16/21:
# PABLO ZABALETA

"I must say he is my favourite player at City, for sure. I love him. I am so lucky to have been playing in the same side as great players but especially David because he is so good.

"It's a pleasure watching him play. He's class, his vision to play football… Probably one of my best seasons at City was when I was overlapping all the time and making runs because I knew the ball would always be there.

"He's fantastic, so special. We are so lucky to have David at Manchester City; he's been fantastic for so many years. Different class. I could keep talking about David all day because I love him so much. For me he's the greatest City player ever."

## #17/21:
## ALVARO NEGREDO

"I like Aguero so much, but my preference is David Silva. People look at the goals; the striker normally draws more passion from the supporters. Aguero scores so many goals. But when you play on the pitch, the striker is important but he doesn't play alone.

"For me, David is the best [in City's history]. When you take a 'number 10' with this quality, this vision, for a striker it's easier. When David takes the ball, you always think 'his pass will come, it will come to me'. Maybe the striker is more egotistical and it's always 'goal, goal, goal', but David is the player who opens the space when the opponent is closed, always the one with the better solution. When I stayed in Manchester, David was the best. And now he continues to be."

## #18/21:
## GARETH BARRY

"I loved playing with David Silva at City.

"When I received the ball, every time I looked up he seemed to be in acres of space."

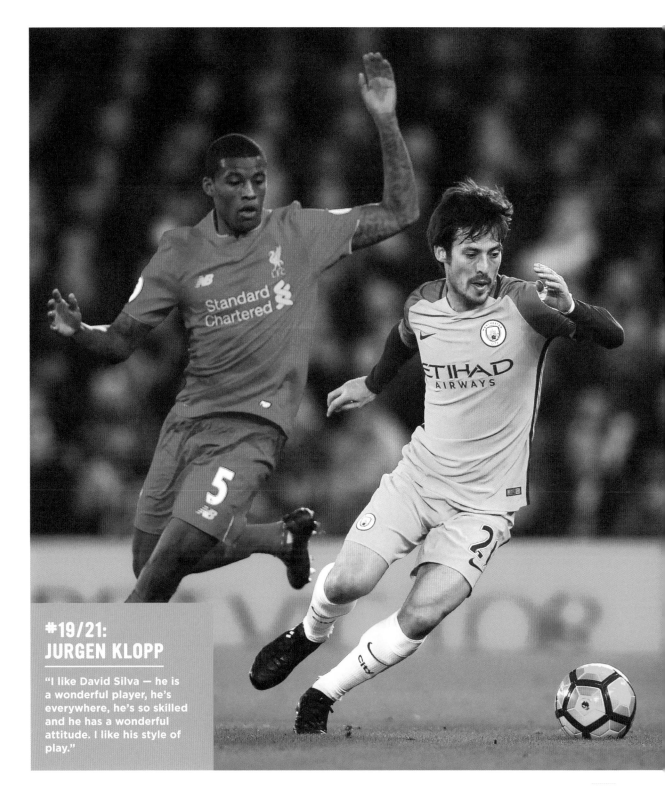

**#19/21:
JURGEN KLOPP**

"I like David Silva — he is a wonderful player, he's everywhere, he's so skilled and he has a wonderful attitude. I like his style of play."

## #20/21:
## BERNARDO SILVA

"He is one of the best midfielders of all-time. David might not score that many goals but he brings something different that maybe people don't always realise — the actions before the goals, he brings so much to the team. It is a different impact he has on the game and it is huge. And maybe that's one of the reasons he didn't have the praise in past seasons that he perhaps should have."

# #21/21:
# BACK TO PEP

"I think it's a matter of survival. When you're not too fast or too strong to play at a high level, you need to stand out. You need to be very, very good. And David is. When I was at Barcelona I'd say: 'How good is this guy? I'd love to have him here.' And at the end of his career we've been together and it's been really good. You've always got those stereotypes... 'He's Canarian, used to the sun, good weather.' And he's coming somewhere so cold.

"But stereotypes aren't good advisors. In my first year at City I'd talk to him about it, how surprised I was that he came here. A league so physical, so tough, so imposing, with this climate, with this style of football. How he was able to survive or adapt and do it so well. That definition, that he's a bit of a 'bastard', is the perfect definition by Mendilibar. You can tell he learnt his football on the street. Like he's threatening, 'There'll only be one winner here.'

"David has that in him and you don't realise it until you get to know him. He is a natural competitor, so the competitiveness of the league was good for him. In the beginning, people might have thought, 'he is so small', — but there are small players and small strong players. But I think it was the way that he protected the ball. The way that he used the ball. The timing of his game. The intelligence that he showed. That kind of alleviated any concerns that people might have about his physical profile for the Premier League.

"He's not interested in giving interviews, social media, Twitter, Instagram, any of that. And it seems that people like David get less recognition than people who do that all day. But I'll tell you something that he does have and that's the respect of his fellow professionals. Of his team-mates, of his rivals, of his managers, of managers he's played against. And he has earned all of that.

"I think that's the dream of every pro, to have the respect of others in their sport. Not what people who don't know you think. Some have all the respect outside, but inside the changing room they have none. David is exactly the opposite and that's the best legacy he could have. And especially in this Club.

"He'll go down in history as one of the top players to ever wear the Man City shirt. If we're talking about the top five, David is one of them. And I don't say that lightly."

# SILVAWARE

Silva is one of the most decorated players in City's history, having lifted many trophies over the past ten years...

## Premier League

| 2012 | 2014 | 2018 | 2019 |
|------|------|------|------|

## FA Cup

| 2011 | 2019 |
|------|------|

## League Cup

| 2014 | 2016 | 2018 | 2019 | 2020 |
|------|------|------|------|------|

## FA Community Shield

| 2011 | 2019 |
|------|------|

245

# Ten of the best

**Silva's City contribution during 10 years of exemplary service...**

## 2010/11
53 games, 6 goals, 14 assists

## 2011/12
48 games, 8 goals, 21 assists

## 2012/13
41 games, 5 goals, 13 assists

## 2013/14
40 games, 8 goals, 16 assists

## 2014/15
42 games, 12 goals, 14 assists

## 2015/16
36 games, 4 goals, 12 assists

## 2016/17
45 games, 8 goals, 11 assists

## 2017/18
40 games, 10 goals, 14 assists

## 2018/19
50 games, 10 goals, 14 assists

## 2019/20*
25 games, 3 goals, 8 assists

*\* Up until time of publication*

# David Silva: 21 facts

**#01/21:**
Has the longest winning streak of any Manchester City player, playing in 23 consecutive victories between August 2017 and March 2018

**#02/21:**
Was Manchester City Player of the Month for a remarkable three consecutive months between October and December 2010

**#03/21:**
He was born on January 8th – the same date as music legend David Bowie

**#04/21:**
He won the same number of caps for his country as legends Roberto Carlos (Brazil) and Peter Shilton (England)

**#05/21:**
In 2011/12, Silva had 15 goal assists, his most ever in a single season

**#06/21:**
He was named in the 2011/12, 2017/18 PFA Team of the Year

**#07/21:**
Manchester City's 3-1 win against Everton in September 2019 saw Silva pick up his 200th Premier League victory in just 289 matches, a new record

**#08/21:**
Has won one Premier League Player of the Month award in September 2011

**#09/21:**
Has made more Premier League appearances for Manchester City than any other player, overtaking Joe Hart (266) during a match with Aston Villa in October 2019

**#10/21:**
Scored the opening goal for Spain in their 4-0 win over Italy in the EURO 2012 final. It was his 18th international goal in his 65th appearance

**#11/21:**
As well as *'El Mago'*, he is nicknamed 'Merlin' for his wizardry on the ball

**#12/21:**
Highest scoring season came in 2013/14 when he scored 12 goals in 42 matches

## DAVID SILVA

**#13/21:**
Silva won his 100th cap for Spain at Euro 2016

**#14/21:**
Was the 2011/2012 and 2016/17 Manchester City Player of the Season

**#15/21:**
Including FA Community Shields, Silva has won 13 major trophies at Manchester City (at the time this book went to press)

**#16/21:**
For his services to Spanish sport, he was granted the Gold Medal of the Royal Order of Sporting Merit in 2011

**#17/21:**
Has never been sent off for Manchester City

**#18/21:**
The players voted for Silva to be the new captain following Vincent Kompany's departure

**#19/21:**
Silva scored after just 52 seconds as City went on to hit eight against Watford in September 2019, including five goals in 18 minutes

**#20/21:**
Retired from international football in August 2018 after 125 appearances for Spain

**#21/21:**
Since his introduction to the Premier League, Silva has more assists than any other player

# Another winner's medal...

It was fitting that David led the team out against Aston Villa in the Carabao Cup final – his fifth League Cup triumph which, along with Sergio Aguero and Fernandinho, is a record shared only with former Liverpool striker Ian Rush.

He had already won the Community Shield as skipper and after the 2-1 triumph over Villa, David later tweeted to almost four million followers, "Great job guys! Another one and that makes five!"

He received a rapturous welcome from the City fans as he left the pitch, but hopefully it won't be the last time he graces the Wembley turf.

As ever, he set the tone for a game that City largely dominated and had one or two half-chances but he couldn't repeat his scoring heroics of the 2019 FA Cup final.

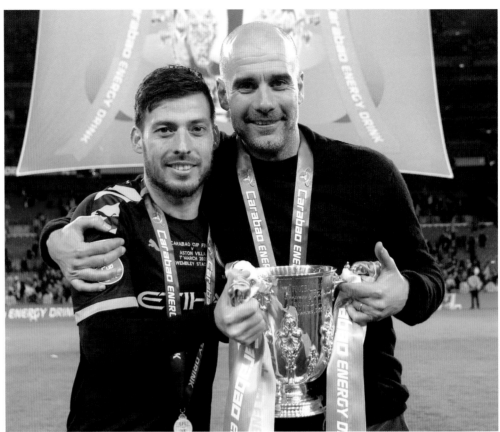

It was his 422nd appearance for the Club, leaving him only a couple away from a place in the Blues' top 10 appearances of all-time list. It was also his 13th winner's medal with Manchester City – no player has won more.

As he humbly led the team up the steps to collect the trophy, he was advised that, as captain, he should wait until the last so he could then lift the Carabao Cup – which he duly did.

As with everything he does, he did it respectfully and with great dignity. Being in the limelight has never been something David particularly enjoys, unless it is because he is playing football. When he is on the pitch, the spotlight is inescapable for this magical footballer.

#21LVA